ODISHA AND SPORTS

ODISHA AND SPORTS

A Story of Hope and Glory

BORIA MAJUMDAR

R. VINEEL KRISHNA

SIMON & SCHUSTER

London · New York · Sydney · Toronto · New Delhi

First published in India by Simon & Schuster India 2024

1 3 5 7 9 10 8 6 4 2

Simon & Schuster India
818, Indraprakash Building,
21, Barakhamba Road,
New Delhi 110001.

Simon & Schuster: Celebrating 100 Years of Publishing in 2024

www.simonandschuster.co.in

Paperback ISBN: 978-81-967547-0-9
eBook ISBN: 978-81-967547-4-7

Typeset in India by SÜRYA, New Delhi
Printed and bound in India by Replika Press Pvt. Ltd.

CONTENTS

FOREWORD

We are on a transformative path towards making Odisha a sports hub and creating a culture of sports among our citizens, especially the youth.
The development of state-of-the-art sports infrastructure in our state stands as a testament to our commitment to nurturing sporting talent. These facilities serve as a platform for not just creating champions in various sports but also to promote health and fitness amongst our youth. We are trying to set benchmarks in organising the national and international championships.

Odisha is today recognised as a global hub for hockey with the best hockey stadiums in the world and organising the Hockey World Cup in 2018 and 2023. We are partnering with national federations, corporates and elite sportspersons to create an eco system of excellence through High Performance Centers in various sports disciplines. We are even partnering with IOC on Olympic

Values Education Program (OVEP) in schools and with FIFA for the Talent Academy.

The vibrant kaleidoscope of sports competitions held on our soil has not only put us on the global sporting map but has also fostered an environment where athletes from diverse backgrounds come together to celebrate the spirit of sportsmanship.

I am delighted to extend my heartfelt congratulations to Mr Boria Majumdar and Mr R. Vineel Krishna, Secretary Sports Odisha, on the release of this insightful book, offering a vivid exploration on the remarkable strides we have taken to transform Odisha into a sporting powerhouse.

As a renowned sports historian and author, Mr Boria Majumdar brings his expertise to unravel the intricacies of our sporting legacy. I commend Mr Majumdar and Mr Krishna for this compelling work and hope it will inspire future generations to embrace the spirit of sports.

NAVEEN PATNAIK
Chief Minister of Odisha

WHEN CHALLENGE BECOMES OPPORTUNITY

From the 90-day challenge to the Birsa Munda Stadium

R. Vineel Krishna

I remember the words of Shri Naveen Patnaik, the Honourable Chief Minister, each time I speak about the 90-day challenge. It was after one of the states had pulled out and the question was asked if we in Odisha wanted to step in at the last minute and host the 22nd Asian Athletics Championships (AAC) in July 2017.

'Many will treat this as an impossible task,' he had said to us then. 'We will treat this as an opportunity.' That's what it was for all of us in Odisha, an opportunity to showcase the state on a global stage. It was our Olympic Games, an opportunity to transform and portray Odisha to the world and, in doing so, ensure that India did not have to give up on the right to host the competition. Little did we know then what was to follow. It actually turned out to be the start of a sporting journey like no other, an adventure that has enriched us all and, in the process, taught us a great deal.

Prohibitive costs and negative legacy in the immediate aftermath has forced the hands of multiple cities, which has made the hosting of mega events a tough task. Most facilities built for such events subsequently turn into unsustainable white elephants. The mega-event caravan moves on and leaves in its trail mammoth facilities with little use for the host city.

Even the Olympics aren't an aberration. Be it the Commonwealth Games or the Asian Games or the Asian Athletics Championships, it is the same story everywhere as far as mega sports events are concerned. Stadiums in Rio, built for the Olympics in 2016, have hardly been used since and the thousands of crores spent on them seem a drain on the country's exchequer. The story is grim. With underdevelopment and a widening gap between the rich and the poor a constant concern, staging mega events has further added to the citizens' growing frustration in some cities.

Should we bid for the AAC? Was such a bid feasible? What trail would the spectacle leave behind? Would it be a legacy of unused facilities or would there be real development with a proper optimisation of costs involved? Could mega events really convert a state into a multi-sporting one, and give it a push like nothing else?. There were multiple concerns at that time of bidding for the event. Odisha has never before hosted an event of this scale. The Stadium was not in good shape to organise this event and there are just 90-days to put together everything including the new athletic tracks, flood lights, upgradation of all facilities of the stadium. All these works to be completed during the peak hot summer season with the probability of a cyclone as well. The event was to be conducted in July which is the peak monsoon season in Odisha. It was a big risk and there were genuine concerns at various levels in the government. Why would Odisha want to take such a huge risk? The Chief Minister was very determined that we should go ahead with the event and show the collective will and dedication of Odisha.

Athletes, most of all, could benefit, and mounting a proper bid might finally herald the turnaround we were looking for. In short, we knew that the success of the AAC would define the story of sporting Odisha in the future.

But while it might sound romantic to start with, organising an event on that scale with a positive legacy wasn't an easy job on ground. Listed prominently in the opportunities section was a clear statement of belief that the event would present the image of Odisha as an emerging sporting hub, and Bhubaneshwar as a global, business-friendly city. Drawing a clear link with Odisha's vocal ambitions of becoming a major sporting powerhouse, the AAC would also help us to highlight the connections between Odisha's sporting history and its recent evolution.

The Kalinga Stadium, now one of the best in the country, with all the modern facilities associated with global sport, was then just a skeleton. During one of our early visits to the stadium soon after the announcement had been made that we would host the Championships from July 5-9, 2017, we found that the stadium was in unusable condition. The drive to the facility was a poor experience, with no proper roads leading to the stadium. The car park was non-existent. The seats in the stands were broken. In fact, I remember the red plastic chairs being either dirty or loose. Lack of maintenance meant the seats were unusable. The flooring inside the stadium was dilapidated and had cracks all over. Waste was strewn around, and it badly needed a complete facelift. In fact, we would need to replace the entire flooring and install new tiles. The stairs were dirty and needed to be redone, and not a single toilet in the entire facility functioned properly. This is a hygiene issue all across India. We need to get better and offer basic hygienic conditions to our spectators. While we take care of the hospitality suites, we tend to neglect the facilities used by the fans. The toilets had to be modernised and cleaned up. And all this in the midst of peak monsoon.

In fact, I remember the last 48 hours leading into the competition. Our teams were all working 24/7 to apply the finishing touches and the opening-ceremony performers were getting ready for their final rehearsals when there was a torrential downpour. Anyone who knows about Odisha would know what I mean. If the rain Gods decide to open up, it can sometimes pour for hours on end. We were looking at the sky and hoping that all the hard work should not go waste because of the weather. The intensity of the shower was such that parts of the final rehearsals had to be called off, and another part had to be done in the rain in plain clothes because we couldn't risk costumes getting wet. In fact, from the first day, we were aware that it was a risk hosting the event at the height of the monsoon. And early July is when the monsoon sets in properly in the state. But then, you don't play for weather as they say, and we had prepared ourselves in every way possible.

In Odisha, we are known for our disaster management initiatives, and this wasn't something that would derail the efforts. More so when the stakes were as high. In the end even the Gods were with us. And with divine blessings, there was no rain on the day of the event. The stadium looked surreal under lights and everything went to plan. Most importantly, the people loved it. Fans watched the event unfold with pride and it was a moment of collective glory. As the teams entered the stadium for the opening ceremony in front of packed stands, each one of us felt a sense of relief and elation. The 90-day challenge was successful. Most importantly, we were able to do it with a buy-in from all our men, women and children. It was Odisha's event in the truest sense of the term.

The backstory

The Asian Athletics Championships were originally awarded to Jharkhand, with the event to be staged in Ranchi. It was only when Jharkhand expressed their inability to host it at the last minute that we got an opportunity to step in. On the advice of Sh Injeti Srinivas, Secretary Sports in Government of India, who belonged to the Odisha Cadre, the Athletics Federation of India approached Odisha with the request. It was Shri V.K. Pandian, Private Secretary to CM, who discussed with the Chief Minister who readily accepted the suggestion. The CM has always looked at sport as a vehicle for change, and for him, it was the perfect way to showcase the work being done in the state. We could use the event to bring our citizens together and with Odisha having a strong tradition in athletics, it seemed a natural fit. What we lacked was infrastructure, and the second step was to get the logistics right. For example, allocation of accommodation to the visiting athletes may seem an insignificant task. But then, you could not put South Korea and North Korea in the same hotel or have Iraq and Iran stay together. These things meant you needed to spend time on hotel allocations and every other detail, and time was the only thing we did not have left. Practice timings for the teams had to be organised in such a way that there was never an issue. Existing political realities were kept in mind when working on the practice roster, and all of this was time consuming.

I remember a day when Vishal Dev, the Sports Secretary, and I were sitting in his office and going through costume designs, which a very well-known fashion-design agency had sent us as samples, for our volunteers. It was already quite late in the day, and we had rejected a few designs that had been sent earlier. The look did not seem right, and neither of us was satisfied. What we had asked for were costumes which highlighted the glories of our local culture. With time running out, we could not afford to go back and forth. We needed a solution, and with immediate effect. With little or no options in sight, the two of us decided to research a number of iconic costumes ourselves, and then created our own design. In the words of Mr. Dev, 'We had to venture into unchartered territory but then we had the will and the determination to do so.' While it was a new learning, it was exciting as well.

When the project was first allocated to us, it seemed a humungous challenge. Everywhere we looked, there was work to be done. And we were told by a number of experts that it wasn't feasible. It wasn't a pragmatic idea to try and take up the challenge. Never had it happened that, in three months, a state had staged an event with 600 athletes from 41 nations, with over 100,000 fans watching across all days. It would be a first, and we needed to break things down for us to have a realistic chance. We needed to calculate backwards, and make a calendar with strict timelines. Only after we had done so did we feel, for the first time, that it could be done. The first thing was to do away with protocol. Each of us had to be hands on 24/7 for those 90 days. And anyone who had a suggestion was welcome to come and share. We were a team with all hands on deck, and there was no hierarchy. We needed to sleep at the stadium to be able to tackle any contingency that came up. And many did. The Kalinga Stadium, in every sense, would be a symbol of Odisha's soft power. It was to showcase what the state stood for, and would counter the narrative that Odisha still had a fair distance to travel to get up to speed with the rest of the country. We decided to hire the best local and national talent, and to source the best equipment available globally. The floodlights were ordered from Italy, and we needed to lay the tracks from scratch. It is a mandatory requirement of the IAAF, now called World Athletics, that you need to have a practice track for any international competition. This too had to be laid.

What we did was divide the work to the minutest detail, and set deadlines for every little thing that had to be done. We had also anticipated that a few unexpected roadblocks could come up, and kept some contingency time on hand. When you embark on a project of such scale, it is always essential to factor in some contingency time. Believe it or not, one of the cranes transporting equipment went missing, and we lost a couple of days. But because we had that little extra time added in, it did not hurt our timelines.

Adille Sumariwala, the President of the Athletics Federation of India, was apprehensive to begin with. 'When I first visited the site, it was all very basic,' he told me. 'A huge amount of work had to be done and construction had to start. With so little time available, deep down I was doubtful how it could all work out.

What really gave me hope was the conviction of the Chief Minister. He seemed steadfast and had a fantastic team on ground.' Just as in cricket, where you plan for small periods of play when batting together in difficult circumstances, we had broken up the 90 days into small blocks. We took stock weekly, and would calibrate if things were going to plan. When you are faced with a stiff target, you don't go into bat thinking you will bat for 90 overs or the entire six hours. Such a thing isn't possible. What the batters do is plan for the next 10 overs. That's what we were doing. The façade of the stadium needed a facelift, and it allowed us to put our creative skills to work.

Having been in administration for decades now, what I can say is that the home stretch is always the most difficult. Just when you think everything is finally under control and you can breathe easy, something calamitous happens. Unless you have anticipated in advance, you are left stranded at the last minute. In our case, it was the weather. While the events could still go on, the opening ceremony and the laser show would get compromised because of the rain. When pitted against the forces of nature, we are still helpless. As God-fearing, simple people who believe in divine blessings, all of us were praying that we be given a chance. And it happened. We did get our opportunity. The rain stopped in time, and everything played out to perfection. To see the smiles on the faces of the athletes was the greatest vindication. Some of our local stars like Srabani Nanda or Purnima Hembram, who had used the stadium for years, couldn't believe the transformation. 'To march in the Indian team jersey in front of our own people in Odisha is the greatest moment of my life,' said Srabani, who took the oath on behalf of the athletes. Purnima too was emotional. 'My parents will never be able to step out of Odisha,' she said. 'For them to see me play, this was the only opportunity. I can't really express what it meant to them.' Athletes from the invited nations were equally satisfied, and some even said that we should host the next edition of the competition as well.

The best words, however, came from General Dahlan Al-Hamad, the leader of the Doha organising committee, hosts of the next edition of the championships. 'Odisha has raised the bar,' he said. To hear General Dahlan say that they would now have to work harder to maintain the standards we had set was the best possible compliment. It had all worked out quite beautifully. The fans had turned up in their thousands and school children had the time of their lives. When the Honourable CM finally said the words, 'Bande Utkal Janani', and declared the meet open, and when Shankar Mahadevan lit up the stadium singing 'Rangabati', we could all look back at a job well done. Not a single person had slept more than four to five hours a day, and the 90-day challenge was easily one of the toughest things we had undertaken. In fact, I wouldn't be wrong to say that had it not been for this challenge, the story of Sporting Odisha would have been different. It was the confidence we all gained from the successful staging of this competition, and the positive legacy it left behind, that prompted us to take the next steps and become more ambitious.

While staging major international competitions was no longer daunting, Covid changed the landscape beyond recognition. It wasn't something the world had seen before and for us in Odisha too, it was a very different and difficult challenge. As a government, protecting our people was the only job we were focussed on. Each of us in administration worked round the clock and while some of us contracted Covid ourselves, at no point did we stop our efforts. And it was in the midst of the pandemic that we staged a second consecutive Hockey World Cup in Odisha in January 2023. If there was anything more difficult than the 90-day challenge, it was that.

This time round, it was a 15-month challenge, with Covid as an added adversary.

The Birsa Munda Stadium and the 15-month challenge

We had staged the Hockey World Cup in Bhubaneshwar in 2018 with much fanfare, and the tournament was an unprecedented success. The tournament started on November 27, and the fans loved the inaugural ceremony which included the biggest and best-crafted drone show ever seen in India. It wasn't a difficult tournament to organise because by November 2018, Bhubaneshwar had every facility needed for hockey. With the entire tournament being held in one city, things weren't too difficult to navigate. Our team had the experience, and it turned out to be a spectacular event.

Even though India lost 1-2 in the quarterfinals to the Netherlands, the eventual finalists, fans attended every game in large numbers, making the tournament the most successful in the history of the FIH [International Hockey Federation]. Odisha was gradually turning into a hub of world hockey, and it was no surprise that in November 2019, the FIH allotted the next World Cup, to be staged in January 2023, to Odisha. Only this time, there was one major difference. The Chief Minister was clear that we couldn't stage it in Bhubaneshwar alone. With Sundargarh being the home of hockey in Odisha, the CM wanted us to host the tournament in Rourkela and Bhubaneshwar. Without Rourkela, there would be no World Cup. That was the mandate. And in Rourkela, a relatively small industrial town in Sundargarh, there was no airport and the number of hotels was inadequate to stage a global event of this scale. Most importantly, there was no stadium for international hockey. There was no practice pitch either. We needed to build the stadium, which had to be the 'Jewel in Odisha's crown'. Nothing else would suffice, and with the tournament coinciding with the 75th anniversary of India's independence, a momentous occasion for the country, the stadium was expected to be Odisha's gift to the nation.

To finish work on a facility that was still in the design stage in just 15 months was a humungous ask. While that timeframe may seem adequate on paper, the ground reality was very different. It was not just 'a' stadium that we had to build. We had to build the world's best hockey stadium, something that everyone in Rourkela and Odisha could be proud of. While doing so, we had to keep in mind that the stadium should also be a kind of public plaza for every citizen of Rourkela. For a large part of the year, it is open to the public, and the locals have access to it and can use it for the perfect evening out with the family.

Just like friends and families go to malls to spend a pleasant evening there watching a film or doing some shopping, special care was taken to build the Birsa Munda Stadium in a manner that provided fans with a similar experience. There are enough grass mounds and banks for people to sit and chat, enough food stalls to munch on snacks, and clean washrooms to use. The idea was not just to build a sports stadium. Rather, it was to create something that would help draw families to the sport. Make for collective recreation. Only then would the children get attracted to the action and aspire to become the stars of tomorrow.

Alongside the main stadium, we also decided to build the World Cup village, a residential facility which could house all the participating teams. It was very similar to an Olympic village, which is a self-sustainable complex. Rourkela did not have the requisite number of hotels, and this was the only way to circumvent the problem. The World Cup village has five blocks, and we started construction on all of them at the same time to make the best use of the available manpower. In doing so, we saved precious time. The blocks are connected by a courtyard, which is the perfect setting for some quality family time in the evenings.

Every international star likes playing at the Birsa Munda Stadium. This is partly because of the excellent residential facilities for players and visitors integrated within the stadium precinct. It means that players don't need to travel long distances and have all the post-game recovery facilities in close proximity. Inaugurated during the World Cup, it allowed players from all the participating teams to reside in the same complex, much like how it is in an Olympic village. Every residential block has multiple indoor sports facilities like table tennis, pool and card games, which helped players relax without having to venture outside. With the experience of the pandemic behind us, it was a conscious plan to make the stadium self-sustainable. In case of an emergency, players could stay and train in the stadium precinct without having to make any outside contact, and every necessity would be readily accessible to them.

The first thing that we worked on was the practice pitch. Construction started on time and we were all hopeful of meeting the September 2022 deadline. Simultaneously, upgradation work had started on the Rourkela airport, with support from the Government of India. With all the teams landing in Rourkela, we needed a better airstrip and everything had to be done in tandem. While the initial deadlines were met, the onset of Covid meant that everything went haywire. We went into complete lockdown, and work came to a standstill. It was only after the world had started to heal a little that we could resume. But supply-chain disruptions continued and the main pitch, to be installed inside the stadium, got delayed. While our workers were all there on site, without the main pitch—which was being imported from Germany—they were all dressed up with nowhere to go. Shipping was a real issue at the time, and one disruption in the supply chain meant that all our timelines had to be recalibrated. We needed all stakeholders to be in sync, and if one part of the chain wasn't working, the entire process was disrupted. During Covid, none of this was in our hands. Other countries had lockdowns too, and the Covid waves hit Europe at various times, triggering very different responses. We needed to compress timelines further to be able to meet the deadline.

To do this, our engineers and experts suggested that we use fabricated steel equipment to build the stands. This would considerably speed up the process without compromising on quality, and was the only option available. But to transport 3000 metric tonnes of fabricated steel to the stadium site was no mean task. These were key to the stadium's look and feel, and had to be used with meticulous care after adequate due diligence. Hundreds of thousands of safe man hours were spent, with teams working round the clock to make up for lost time. But not once did the workers complain. They were all part of the extended family and realised the importance of the task at hand. In fact, a lot of them stayed on site, and were itching to get going with each passing day.

If it was Covid to begin with, in 2022 we also had a very bad monsoon to add to the enormity of the challenge. For days, the rain did not stop, and as Bhupinder Poonia, IAS, MD IDCO, who was in charge of the construction, said, 'For a period, the outdoor work had to be stopped completely. You couldn't take a risk in inclement weather, and the workers' safety was paramount. Even when they wanted to resume, we had to hold them back until we were given an all-clear from the team.'

Work on the main stadium façade was further delayed because of this. While the practice facility was completed and inaugurated in September 2022 by delegates from the FIH and Hockey India, we decided to extend the final timelines for the main stadium by three months. We knew we were cutting it fine, but with Covid and heavy extended monsoons, there was little we could do under the circumstances. December was a hard deadline, with some teams planning to make their way to Odisha by then. Whatever happened, that timeline had to be met. Shaun Goudie, who was laying the turf, stepped up with his team the moment the main pitch arrived from Germany, and completed the work in no time. And with the north, south and east stands all complete, only the west stand was left to be finished. In the meantime, the floodlights were also installed, and each step was completed depending on the requirements of the FIH and the broadcast crews. There are eight masts in the Birsa Munda Stadium, and each is a marvel of technology. Every part of the stadium needed to be lit uniformly and the first day the lights were all switched on, we couldn't stop smiling.

The West stand was critical because it was from there that the teams would make their way on to the field of play. It was the main entrance, and would be the most used. The façade was of extra significance because that was what the world would see during the broadcast. If you remember the football World Cup in Qatar, that was what left those watching in awe. We wanted something similar with the Birsa Munda Stadium in Rourkela. As Shri Pandian said, 'The Chief Minister is very particular about architecture, and paid personal attention to the colour coding used in the façade. He allowed the creative teams to present the designs, and then a final call was taken.' By late December, everything seemed in place and the final touches were being given. Checks were being carried out regularly to ensure that every facility was working, and we were all finally gearing up for the inauguration.

But like in the case of the 90-day challenge, something unexpected had to happen. If it was the rain in 2017, it was fog in December-January 2022-23. Fog has been a persistent problem in winters in eastern India, and there was very little we could do about it. Despite having a newly laid airstrip in the city, flights couldn't take off for days because of the heavy fog. It meant that we needed to arrange for additional transport from Rourkela to Jharsuguda, and then organise flights from there. Just to put things into context, this wasn't about transporting one or two people. Teams had to travel between the two cities, and it presented a major logistics challenge because the schedule couldn't be altered at the last minute. When running against deadlines, this was an additional headache to deal with. But by then, we had become immune to such pressures. We knew we had to get the work done, come what may, and no challenge was insurmountable.

Support from Hockey India and the FIH helped along the way, and when Thierry Weil, the CEO of FIH, said on the day of the inauguration of the practice pitch that he was sure we would complete everything on time, it gave us all a big boost. 'When you enter the stadium, you realise that the drawings that were presented to us were all accurate,' said Weil in September 2022. 'The scale is gigantic. While it is not finished yet, the number of people working and the efficiency with which they are doing it, I am sure all will be done on time.'

Finally, in January 2023, the Chief Minister was there

to inaugurate the facility. We had worked till the very last day, and almost till the very last minute. The Chief Minister was fully satisfied with what we had achieved, and each of us felt immense pride at the accomplishment. I am not exaggerating when I say that the Birsa Munda Stadium is the best hockey facility in the world, a sentiment shared by a galaxy of stars led by our very own PR Sreejesh—one of India's greatest-ever players.

'Let me say this emphatically—it is the most spectacular hockey facility I have played in,' said Sreejesh. 'Every detail has been taken care of, and the very aura of this majestic facility leaves a mark on you. Jhakaas, as they say. It's rare to have a hockey stadium that seats 20,000 people, and that's what makes the Birsa Munda special. With the World Cup village aligned with it, we could reach the main venue within minutes, further adding to players' comfort.

'In fact, I can comfortably say that players from across the world want to come and play in the Birsa Munda Stadium. This is because each one of us want to perform in front of packed crowds in a facility like this. They will encourage you all through, and even if you don't get the desired result, they will stand by you and support you. Even after we lost to New Zealand in the World Cup in January 2023, the kind of support we received in Rourkela during our classification matches was unrivalled. I can tell you that, as a player, I just love playing at the Birsa Munda.'

It was a transformation of Rourkela as a major hockey hub with a Guinness Record for the largest seated hockey stadium in the World. In the words of the Secretary 5T, Sh V K Pandian, 'We did not have a stadium in Rourkela. Not even a skeleton. We did not have an airport. We did not have adequate good accommodation for players. We did not have good connectivity. And all we had was 15 months. What we did have was will and determination. We had our CM's vision that we had to do this for Sundargarh and Rourkela. And most importantly, we had the people of Sundargarh standing with us every step of the way. It was for them that we managed to pull this off. The Birsa Munda is truly an architectural marvel, and a jewel in Odisha's crown.'

Since the World Cup, the stadium has been used for multiple local tournaments and camps, and is now well integrated within the city's sports culture. In fact, the young hockey talents who are all part of the Panposh Sports Hostel in Rourkela have access to the facility, and that will only make them better players. These youngsters are the future of hockey in the state, and torch-bearers of a tradition that has been Odisha's pride for decades now.

A VISIONARY LEADER AND A SPORTING DREAM

Crafting a new Odisha

Odisha has forever been a favourite destination for many of us growing up in Bengal. My first memory of Odisha is my father telling me that a puja vacation was incomplete without going to Puri and Bhubaneshwar. In fact, it was a ritual. Every puja we would go to the neighbouring state for a good two weeks. It was affordable and quick and, may I say, thoroughly enjoyable. I loved visiting the Jagannath Temple and having the *prashad* within the temple precinct was the highpoint of the tour. Few things taste so delicious and the experience of sitting down with fellow Indians trying out the *prashad* was really humbling.

Every evening, we would go to the beach. Take long walks and then end up sitting down in one of the shacks for a fresh seafood meal. The *pujo* in Puri is the perfect Bengali holiday.

It was not just about Puri. Going to the Lingaraja and Mukteshwar Temples in Bhubaneshwar, buying Sambalpuri silk sarees for my mother and a few kurtas for friends and family, buying kilos of the *gaja*—a favourite sweet to take back home—are all memories of a lifetime.

Then there was Konark. An architectural marvel, no visit to Konark was complete without taking a few hundred pictures of the intricate carvings, which till date remain one of the wonders of the world. To see the Konark wheels now being discussed in the G20 summit is a matter of great pride.

But in all this, there was no sport. Odisha and sport did not go hand in hand then. Rather, locals from Odisha would travel to Bengal to play and it was not something which was a priority in Odisha. There were a few local stars, Dilip Tirkey and Lazarus Barla to name two, who made it to the national team, but these were all individual efforts rather than results of any form of structural change in the state.

Now things are different. Under the leadership of one of India's most-loved and admired Chief Ministers, Shri Naveen Patnaik, Odisha has turned the page, and how. With the amount of work that has happened in the last six years, the state is now the new nerve centre of Indian sport. With the most incredible infrastructure and the best technical expertise and coaching, Odisha has started to produce some incredible athletes who end up scripting some incredible stories of achievement.

Take the case of Sundargarh, for example. Not too long ago, it was a tribal belt with little or no facilities for sport. People in Sundargarh played hockey and some like Dilip Tirkey made it to the Indian team from the pebbled fields in the district but such stories were more of 'jugaad' than anything else. Dilip was an aberration and not the norm. And there were a few like him making Sundargarh the cradle of hockey in Odisha. But without a structure in place, you can only go up to a certain point and no more. The Indian hockey story is proof. Once the dominant global force in field hockey, India has not won a major championship for decades and it was only in Tokyo after a gap of 41 years that the Indian team was back on the Olympic podium. A degree of credit for this showing goes to what has been done in Odisha in the past few years.

In Bengal, a state which is bigger than Odisha, there is one turf pitch for hockey. It isn't there yet and is being installed as this book is being written. In the Sundargarh district alone, there are 22 artificial turfs with more on the way. Odisha has hosted close to 25 international sports and national events of scale in the last five years. No state has hosted more than half of it. No country has hosted back-to-back hockey World Cups in decades while Odisha managed to do so successfully in 2018 and 2023. More recently, we have started to see Odisha make a mark on the international stage with a slew of its athletes starting to win medals or producing their personal bests. Kishore Jena in javelin is one such example. With Neeraj Chopra dominating the sport in India, not many had heard of Jena ahead of the Budapest World Championships. Having qualified with a throw of 84 metres, Jena was brilliant at the biggest stage of all to make the final and finish fifth. Coming into his own at a relatively mature age of 29, Jena is proof what proper coaching and sports science can do for an athlete.

And it's not just Jena. In someone like Hupi Majhi, not to forget the likes of Dumini Marndi and Mama Naik, we have some of the best examples of women's empowerment. Both Majhi and Marndi are from underprivileged backgrounds where two square meals were once considered a luxury. No one in their respective villages had ever travelled in an airplane or ever heard of social media. Farming was all they knew and for the women, life ended with marriage. Girls weren't allowed to wear shorts in the village and playing with boys or men was considered disrespectful. To come to terms with a woman playing a body contact sport was a far cry.

'To have one extra glass of milk or one extra roti was a luxury,' said one of the rugby girls when we spoke to them. 'It meant my mother would have go to hungry that night.' Now, things are different. Rugby and the facilities on offer in Odisha have given them lives of respect and comfort. They have started to earn reasonable monies and when the government of Odisha announced five lakh rupees for making the Indian team in 2017, it was considered a windfall for the entire village. All of a sudden, the social taboos were broken and Majhi was considered the role model for every aspiring youngster. Now the government has announced a further 10 lakh rupees for every athlete from the state who is part of the Asian Games, and such gestures will only further help the growth of sport in the future. Ask Majhi the marriage question and you get the best answer, 'The choice is between doing something for India and getting married,' she said. 'I don't think the question is relevant anymore.'

Each of these extraordinary athletes who all have extraordinary stories now have the infrastructure needed to hone their talent. A visit to the Kalinga Stadium complex and suddenly you are transported to the developed West. Rather, there is nothing like this in the world at the moment and Odisha has clearly taken the lead in producing the best multi-sport precinct that there exists in India. With the manicured lawns welcoming you to the complex, all one needs to do is just park the car in the car park adjacent to the hockey stadium and walk in. The Kalinga Hockey Stadium is one of the best in the world and only second to the Birsa Munda Stadium in Rourkela in capacity. Sitting in the media centre, one wonders why India can't produce cricket stadiums, which are even half as good. The best index are the washrooms. Cricket, which has way more money than any other sport in India, still lacks in fan experience and the washrooms in most stadiums tell a story. During match days, they are unusable. Overflowing with piss, these toilets aren't the best advertisement for what Indian cricket can offer. Move to hockey and the Kalinga Stadium and it is the ultimate fan experience of sorts. Clean toilets, proper Wi-Fi, fantastic facilities for the media and adequate food stalls for the fans, it is the perfect fan experience for anyone interested in the sport. For players, it is one of the best venues to play in and the location of the hockey stadium means players must walk 20 metres to get to the sports science facility for recovery.

The Sports Science High Performance Centre in the Kalinga Stadium complex, done in collaboration with the Abhinav Bindra Foundation, is the best state of the art sports science facility in the country. With every modern machine that can aid athletes' recovery and injury management, it offers Indian athletes the best means to recuperate and get ready for a major competition. Other sports, which all have high performance centres housed in the same precinct are athletics, football, swimming, shooting, gymnastics and weightlifting. The country's biggest and best indoor athletics stadium is also complete, further adding to the gloss of this ever-growing sports hub.

But then it is not just about Bhubaneshwar. In fact, it was a clear diktat from the Chief Minister that Odisha could only host the 2023 Hockey World Cup if it was staged in Rourkela and not just in the state capital alone. With Covid coming in between, impacting timelines and supply chain issues, building the Birsa Munda Stadium and the adjoining World Cup village in time for the World Cup was one of the most difficult challenges the administrators in Odisha have ever undertaken. With things not always in their control, they had to work round the clock 24/7 to get the stadium ready in time for the showpiece event in January 2023.

It isn't wrong to say that while India did not win the hockey World Cup, Odisha certainly did. The fans and the organisers did. Over 20,000 fans watching hockey in the Birsa Munda Stadium was a sight to behold and it was a statement that Odisha as a state with sports at its heart has well and truly arrived. The World Cup was a spectacle of the highest order and brought the fans closer to the action than ever before. Most importantly, the fans in Odisha don't just watch the sport. Rather, they play it in numbers explaining the 75 hockey internationals the state has produced.

With 90 multi-purpose indoor stadiums, 25 hockey training centres, 314 rural mini stadiums and 149 urban mini stadiums and a budget of 1300 crores earmarked for sport, the Odisha sports revolution is well and truly underway. With the best of corporate India coming together in partnering with the government in setting up the High Performance Centres across the state, it is now a model that is being emulated in different parts of India. With athletes winning medals and making a mark, things can only get better in the future from here on.

'In Odisha, they have managed to get it right,' said Rahul Bose, President of Rugby India and one of India's best-known actors. 'The best thing is there is no red tape. If you have a genuine proposal all you need to do is to take it to the Chief Minister and you know there is support and empathy no questions asked. What more can you ask for as an administrator?'

From according equal status and prize money to athletes with disability and making sure women aren't left behind in this growth story, Odisha is Indian sport's best-kept secret.

'The narrative for the longest time has been one of

negativity,' argues R. Vineel Krishna, my co-author and Secretary Sports, Government of Odisha. 'If you see every Olympic Games from 1976 onwards, it is always about 100 crore Indians and these few medals. The Chief Minister wanted to change it. Using sport as a means to showcase the work done in the state, Shri Naveen Patnaik was determined to add to the Indian sports story. That's why we decided to sponsor the men's and women's hockey teams, the women's rugby team and athletes from many other disciplines. Sport is an example of soft power and helps unite the people while also bringing about a kind of lifestyle change that nothing else is really capable of. For us in Odisha, it is not just about elite high-performance sport. Rather, it is also about the grassroots and sport for all. That's when real development happens.'

Best to leave the closing words to Dilip Tirkey, one of the biggest sports stars to have come out of Odisha. 'It is a story like no other,' says Tirkey. 'As a young boy growing up in Sundargarh, all we had was passion for the sport. There were no facilities and no money. In the absence of support, a lot of our talented young boys and girls did not pursue sport. Talent never met opportunity in India at the turn of the millennium. Now it is different. For every talented youngster in Odisha, there are facilities on offer to hone that talent. Things have changed and how. It almost seems like a fairytale at times. But then, it is real, not reel, and that's the best part about this Odisha story.'

This book is the story behind the story. How it all happened and what the end goal is. The story of a sporting Odisha and how it aspires to become the home of Indian sport. By no means is it over yet, and that's what makes documenting this journey that much more interesting.

It is the story of a state, and how it has used sport to make change. United its people, and created infrastructure that makes a huge difference.

Here's a story.

It was the morning of July 12, 2023, and I happened to be at the newly established Gymnastics High Performance Stadium in the Kalinga Stadium precinct. The Asian Games trials had just ended and the athletes were all relaxing at the end of two hard days. A number of journalists were hovering around taking a few quotes and people were relaxed all round. That's when a few of the cleaners walked in. They started picking up every piece of scrap paper lying around and I was curious what they were speaking about. Odiya is pretty close to Bangla as a language and I tried getting close to them to understand the conversation.

'It is our responsibility to ensure the facility stays this way in the months to come,' said one of them to a young man who had joined that morning. 'The government has spent crores in building them. But then, if we don't maintain it, things will not be the same in six months. This is our state and it is important we do our bit in making the state proud of what we have. We might not have the money to make a difference. But in our own way, we can contribute to the state and the effort being put in.' And as he said so, he was presented with a t-shirt by Ashok Mishra, the Gymnastics Head Coach. 'For all the hard work you have put in,' said the coach while handing it over.

In that one instant, I could sense why Odisha is different. The Odisha sports story isn't about the government anymore. Nor is it about the athletes. It is the people's story with heart at the centre of it. This book is their story.

OLYMPIC VALUE EDUCATION PROGRAMME (OVEP) IN ACTION

Making a difference and making a better world

There were no cameras. No media. It was all rather quiet as Abhinav Bindra and an International Olympic Committee (IOC) delegation led by Angelita Teo, Director of the Olympic Foundation of Culture and Heritage, made it to one of the 90 pilot schools under the Olympic Values Education Programme (OVEP) in Bhubaneshwar on April 3, 2023. With the mercury touching 37 degrees, it wasn't pleasant. The moment we stepped out of the air conditioning, we sweated profusely. Day-long outdoor activities with school kids in sapping heat did not seem an enticing prospect. In fact, someone could have felt unwell. And yet, all of us were there with Abhinav, to see what was happening with this partnership between the Government of Odisha and the Abhinav Bindra Foundation. Could sport truly change lives? Could the Government of Odisha, Abhinav and the IOC make a difference to the lives of 150,000 young girls and boys using sport and the values associated with it? Could they scale things up even further, as was now the case, and make this an all-India engagement going forward?

As we reached the school, the delegation was welcomed in the traditional Indian way—with flowers and conch shells. That was routine. But it was then that things started to get interesting. The kids, from economically underprivileged backgrounds all across the state, were smartly dressed in well-ironed school uniforms, and had lined up to welcome the delegation. There was a certain warmth about the whole thing. Each child was smiling and seemed to be soaking up everything going on around them. And as we took our seats in front of the temporary stage, two students—a boy and a girl—walked up to the dais and welcomed us in perfect English. They were addressing a crowd of over 200, which included senior IOC delegates from Switzerland. They mentioned what they had planned, and how sport had made them more confident individuals. The high point of this opening ceremony was when two girls came down from the stage, and held Angelita and Xenia Kourgouzova—Senior Manager, Education, IOC—by the hand, asking them to join the students on the dais for a traditional Odia dance. That might have seemed silly to some. But if you thought a little deeper, the symbolism would not have been lost on you. These were students who had little or no exposure to the world a year or so earlier. English was an alien language for them. No one in their families had ever spoken in English, let alone interacted with foreigners in the language. And here, out of the blue, two of the girls had the confidence to come down and invite two senior IOC delegates on to the stage. A revolution was unfolding in front of our eyes, and Odisha, India's best-kept secret, felt like a new ray of hope.

The welcome performance was followed by a uniquely planned game of football. Two teams of six a side each were pitted against each other, with three players instructed not to go beyond the halfway line. The teams, interestingly, had three boys and three girls on each side. 'Some of the boys could be better players at the moment, but that's not relevant here,' said a senior teacher at the school. 'We have stopped them from going beyond the halfway line, because that means they have to pass the ball to their teammates to be able to score. That's what will help unite them as a team. Individual efforts don't matter. And by passing to their female counterparts, they will learn to respect each other more. Over a period of time, some girls have become as good, if not better, than the boys, and are now leaders of their teams.'

The significance of that wasn't lost on Abhinav. 'This is one of the biggest successes of the programme,' he said. 'In some cases, boys have chosen girls as leaders, and I can tell you that has given me the most joy.'

'I was apprehensive about playing football,' one of the girls told us. 'I was told it was a game for boys only. And then one day, I fell and injured myself. My parents were scared what might happen to me. But my teachers and trainers under OVEP encouraged me to keep going. Today, I love football. I just love it. I am playing for a club, and if I can do well, I want to play the sport professionally.'

Her eyes sparkled as she spoke to us, and she ended the conversation by asking: 'Do you want me to juggle the ball?'

This was a 14-year-old tribal girl from interior Odisha saying that she was happy to juggle a football 100 times, without it touching the ground, in front of complete strangers. While she wasn't able to control it after 56 touches and was left a little frustrated as a result, she left us all in awe.

As she spoke, I could see Abhinav's eyes light up. He was listening intently, soaking in every word. From shooting for Olympic gold to watching mixed-gender football being played by tribal kids in Bhubaneshwar was quite a journey. It compelled me to ask him why. How did it all start, and how did he end up being here?

'The credit goes to the Government of Odisha,' he said. 'Had it not been for the support we have received from the Chief Minister and everyone else in Odisha, we could not have gone ahead. For me, sport is about values. Life lessons. Not about medals won. Yes, the Olympic gold medal has its importance, and it has helped me hugely, but it is not something I wear around my neck every day. It doesn't define who I am. What sport has helped me to do is bring about change. It has helped me to change as well. That's what I have tried to bring about here in Odisha. It has been possible because there is a certain spontaneity here. You see it in the bureaucracy. They are ready to help you, embrace change, and try out new things. If sport can help change lives and make better societies, I would say my 22 years in sport have been of some significance.'

Could a programme like OVEP change long-established stereotypes? Could it, for example, help give physical education (PE) teachers in India the same respect and credibility that a maths or science teacher got? When growing up in Kolkata, we had a period in school titled, 'Socially Useful Productive Work'. We conveniently changed the name to 'Some Useful Periods Wasted'. It defined our mentality, and what we thought of physical education and PE teachers. Could OVEP help change that mindset in Odisha?

'Yes, that's what it has done for me,' said Rachita, a PE teacher in one of the participating schools. 'Since I became a part of OVEP, I have been able to work far more closely with the other teachers. They are also using sport in their classes to help change the mindset of the students. There is far more synergy. Much more than theory, what is helping us drive change is the more practice-driven approach. We do a lot of outdoor activities with students and that helps them bond better, respect each other more, and be more open with each other.'

'It has made education more exciting,' said a senior teacher who now uses references from OVEP to make her classes more exciting. 'It is not just about reading and being confined to classrooms. It is about mingling with each other outdoors, playing sport, and getting educated while doing so. All of a sudden, school has become exciting. It is not a compulsion. Rather, the students are excited about coming to school and trying out things.'

Clearly, teachers too were now part of the revolution. For them as well, it was a story of empowerment. 'Earlier, we as physical education teachers were always the second rung,' said a PE teacher actively involved in the programme. 'We did not have the same respect in school. Now, things are different. We are, thanks to the OVEP programme, as much respected and well regarded. Our work is getting recognised, and we can see how much the kids are loving it.'

By then, the football was over, and the kids made their way to the sand art, which had been prepared for the IOC delegation. It is an Odisha tradition, and has a long history to it. Again, it was done using the same principles of friendship, respect and excellence. 'What is striking here is how the teachers and students are working in perfect synergy in the state using sporting values,' said Angelita. 'That's what Olympism and the Olympic movement is all about. If we can touch lives like this with sport all over Odisha, we will request Abhinav to take the programme to every corner of India. Odisha is the perfect case study for the IOC.'

Frederique Jamolli, Head International Cultural Affairs, IOC, and Kourgouzova, were both in agreement. 'The Olympic Games is unique because it is a movement, and not just a sports competition that is held every four years,' they argued. 'In fact, what is done in between the four years is what defines Olympism and the Olympic movement.'

In sport, you always fail in public. In front of millions.

Even the great Sachin Tendulkar did so in the 2007 World Cup, when he was out for a duck in the all-important group fixture against Sri Lanka. He wanted to retire after defeat in that game knocked India out of the tournament. Thankfully, he did not. As Abhinav says, 'Sport teaches you to fail.' Tendulkar came back, with his support system backing him up, and won the World Cup in 2011. Again, with millions watching.

That's what makes sport unique. It's perhaps the only human endeavour that allows you to fail in public, and then come back and win in front of the same audience. And that's what Abhinav and his team were teaching the 150,000 young girls and boys in Odisha. Equipping the children to deal with failure. To lose, and come back stronger. To not lose hope and be invested in the process. Despite all the negativity and toxicity in India at the moment, OVEP was all about emphasising how friendship, respect and excellence could help bring about change. And that's where Odisha led the way.

The journey with OVEP has just started in Odisha. We have only seen a year of it. But from what we have witnessed so far, it is a very powerful tool for change. And for a true devotee of sport like Abhinav, it is an opportunity. To try and create a better India. Impact lives. And knowing him well, it is safe to say that he will. With fantastic support from the Odisha government and the Chief Minister in particular, this is a partnership that will only become stronger in the years ahead.

Just as Sydney 2000 and Athens 2004 prepared Abhinav for Beijing 2008, Odisha is readying him for a much bigger canvas. Only this time, it is not him and his gun. It is Abhinav and thousands of underprivileged Indian kids who would otherwise struggle for a respectable living. From families that never dared to dream. It is for them that Abhinav must hit the bullseye. For his sake, and for each of these kids. For, that's what sport has taught him. Odisha is now his range, with thousands of parents watching with bated breath to see how their kids can become more well-rounded individuals. No Olympic gold could match the satisfaction if he can pull it off.

Capital High School Unit 3: A visit to remember

'The football match will be in Capital High School Unit 3,' said Karan Singh, project lead at the Abhinav Bindra Foundation. 'You are welcome to attend. Abhinav, Angelita, Frederique and Xenia from the IOC will also be there.' For them, it was part of the scheduled visit. For me, it meant missing an IPL show and other important work. Should I bother with a local football match? It couldn't be anything that I hadn't seen before, especially since it was being played at a neighbourhood school.

That was when Abhinav stepped in and said, 'Come, for you won't regret it.' Dipta Mishra, the Sports Communications Lead for the Government of Odisha, now a close friend, gave the final push. 'You should experience it,' she said. 'Trust me, you won't mind missing an IPL game.'

With all that persuasion, I decided to give the IPL show a miss and accompany them to the game.

I was glad I did.

First of all, the facility was a real surprise. Located in a bylane of Bhubaneshwar, it is an international standard facility. 'Teams used it during the U-17 FIFA World Cup,' said one of the teachers. A full-size football pitch with excellent changing rooms and a residential hostel attached to it, the facility was the first eye-opener of the evening. And it was not just the pitch. The stands on either side were beautifully done up, and it was noticeable just how clean they were. Unlike many other facilities in India, this one stood out because of its maintenance.

'This is not the only school with such facilities,' said one of the senior teachers, her eyes full of pride. 'Rather, this is now a model all across the state. The government has invested serious money and effort to make these facilities available to talented kids all across the state.'

When the teams lined up, my interest piqued. They were both mixed-gender sides, with girls making up half the number of players. It was the first of many pleasant surprises.

As the match started, a couple of the girls made an immediate impact. They were as good as the boys, and one could see the kind of talent that there is in India. 'We now have 450 students staying in the hostel,' said the PE teacher pointing towards the residential facility located just beyond the stadium compound. 'And more and more girls are now taking to sport, and wanting to be a part of the Olympic Values Education Programme.'

'OVEP has given these boys and girls a new lifeline,' said the Headmaster of the Capital School, which had sport facilities that were used by Indian Super League (ISL) clubs for training. 'It is a way of thinking alien to many of us. It helps integrate sport in all that we do and, in doing so, builds character. Mixed-gender teams are a prime example.' To see girls and boys play football together was an incredible experience. Not only did the girls match the boys in skill and enthusiasm, some of them even assumed leadership roles on the field. They now stay in residential halls and have a life of their own. 'You can see the change,' continued the Headmaster. 'We have an entrance test for students wishing to enrol in the programme. For every 100 entrants, we have 400 applications. Everyone now wants to be a part of it.'

It was at the insistence of the headmaster that I visited

the hostel. I had been to many hostels in my life, and that included several beyond Indian shores. Trust me when I say that I had found few that were as clean. I was allowed inside the students' rooms and was pleasantly surprised to see how neatly things were kept. The corridors were clean and the toilets were not a health hazard, a common feature in almost all Indian hostels. The stairs weren't stained with gutkha, and there was a certain freshness to the whole place that made you feel welcome.

Angelita too seemed overwhelmed by what she saw. 'I had heard a lot about the Odisha model and the work being done,' she said. 'But it is one thing to hear something, and another to come and see for yourself. What I have seen has exceeded my expectations. I will take it back to the IOC, and we will back the project on an even bigger scale.'

Just as Angelita was about to tell me more, she paused and jumped up. The first goal had been scored, and the way it was celebrated by the boys and girls together was the success of the project playing out in front of our eyes. There were high fives all round, and one of the girls was seen instructing the boys to be more attentive in defence, saying she would be there to shield them if needed so that they could play with complete freedom. It was a first for me, in all my years of covering sport.

Kourgouzova, who had visited Odisha before, put

it rather well. 'I am pleased that teachers have included sport and integrated the values of OVEP into teaching other subjects,' she said. 'We aren't here to just promote sport. It is not about who wins or loses. It is about respect, friendship and excellence. And each is as important as the other. You can now see each of these values being integrated into programmes here, giving us all a lot of satisfaction.' And after a second's pause, she added: 'The programme is for them, and by them. That's the beauty of it. It is about what works, and what benefits a society most. We are facilitators. Ultimately, it is about the students who are part of it. What gives us enormous satisfaction at the International Olympic Committee is to see such a great impact in such a short time.'

By then, the match was over. And true to the spirit of the project, it ended in a 1-1 draw. As we were about to leave, two of the children walked up to Abhinav and Angelita. 'We have watched you on TV,' they said in excellent English. 'Now, we are seeing you in front of us. It is a dream fulfilled.' Abhinav, overwhelmed, turned to us and said, 'They are a dream I am living. My true sporting legacy.'

For me, it was indeed an evening well spent.

Government Girls High School Unit 4

As I left for Kolkata on April 3, 2023, overwhelmed by what I had seen in Bhubaneshwar, there was just one doubt. And this stemmed from being in the media for two decades. We are always conditioned to doubt things, even what we observe with our own eyes. We're taught to probe a little more. Was all that I had seen earlier in the day a regular affair, or had it been staged because the IOC and Abhinav were visiting? Had the school put on a show for us? Could it have been organic and spontaneous, or was there an effort to dress things up for the high-profile international delegation visiting the school?

These were uncomfortable, but important, questions. I needed answers to be doubly sure of the impact I had seen. The only way to do this was to visit another school with my team, and arrive unannounced. We would give no prior intimation, and just land up in order to see the ground reality on a regular school day. With the IPL on in April-May and a visiting Professorship at the Neoma Business School in Paris lined up for June, I decided to do this in July, with the RevSportz core team traveling with me. There was enough time and distance between April and July, and the school we chose would have no chance to put on a production if no one was informed of our impending visit.

We identified the Government Girls High School Unit 4, not the most well-endowed or high profile—a regular school with very modest facilities. The choice was made on the basis of a list we had been provided. We randomly chose the school and decided to go ahead with the visit. It was a completely random selection, and that way, it made for a perfect case study. If we could see real transformation on the ground in a school such as this, all our apprehensions would be dispelled.

We reached the school at exactly 11 a.m. on July 17, 2023. It had rained that morning, and that made us all a little apprehensive. If there was rain around, what would be the condition of the school ground, and how would the students be out there playing? Thankfully, by 10 a.m. the showers had come and gone, and the sun was out. The security guard at the gate was a little taken aback to see so many visitors wanting to meet the school management, especially since we were not on any list that had been provided. It was only after a little persuasion that I was allowed to go and meet the school's Principal, who was relatively new, having taken charge just a few months earlier.

This was even better. She couldn't have seen all that had transpired in the past year, and would be able to tell us only about the ground reality as it was that day. To my surprise, the Principal was most cordial. The moment

I said I wanted to speak about OVEP and interact with the students, she readily agreed. It was the first sign that the programme was working in an organic way. There was absolutely no hesitation, and within a minute, she had asked the security to let my entire team in after we had shown them our press cards.

'Hum log ek cup chai pi lete hain. Tab tak aap ka team school dekh le [We shall drink a cup of tea. Till then, let your team see the school],' she said, brimming with confidence. 'Our school now has smart classrooms, and the students have access to all of it,' she added, while looking at multiple CCTV screens on her computer. 'As we speak, a drill is going on, which you can go and check. It is a mixed-gender drill, and we also get our students to play football together. It really helps them.'

This was a government school, mind you.

Just then, Sharmistha, co-founder of Revsportz and an ardent advocate of women's empowerment, walked in with a smile. 'You should go and see it,' she told me. 'Girls and boys playing mixed kho-kho together, and another lot learning football skills. Even the way the field is maintained is something fantastic. The walls have graffiti from the Olympics, and each one is clean and well-curated. We don't normally see things like this in a government school. This is fantastic for all the students.'

The principal had a smile on her face and, all of a

sudden, the tea tasted sweeter. It was April 3rd all over again, and this time, I had no reason to doubt whether it had been staged. As I went up to one of the classrooms, it was fascinating to see kids, who had perhaps never seen a computer before, working on the machines and scrolling through the library catalogue for books.

The best, however, was yet to come.

As we went into the OVEP room, with charts and paintings all over the walls, we happened to ask two young girls what 'Olympic Value Education' meant to them, and what they had learned under OVEP. Neither could have been more than 11 or 12 years old. When I think back to my own school days, I have to say that I would have been overawed. If a few outsiders had come to school and abruptly started quizzing me about things, I wouldn't have been comfortable. My daughter, who is nine and goes to La Martiniere for Girls, one of the best schools in Kolkata, would have been unnerved. It often takes a little bit of time for kids to be comfortable, and that's natural.

Here, things were profoundly different. The two young students were relaxed and greeted us warmly. Without any hesitation, one of them introduced herself and then her friend before she started to explain what OVEP meant to her. 'It teaches us friendship, respect and excellence,' she said. 'And it will help us become better human beings and support each other better.

Under OVEP, we are taught values and also taught that more than winning or losing, what is most important is teamwork and fair play…'

All I could do was watch and listen in complete amazement.

When I asked one of the girls what their families thought about OVEP, her reaction was startling. 'My father is an auto driver,' she said. 'In our family, girls weren't encouraged to play sport. My mother works as a cook, and it hasn't been easy. But when I said to my father that I wanted to attend school and play, he did not say no to me. He asked how it would benefit me, and how I could help at home. But now, after a year, he keeps asking me to speak English each time I go home. He doesn't understand much, but just wants to hear me speak. For him, his daughter speaking English is a matter of great pride. I am the first person in my family who can understand and speak English.'

She said all this in a very matter-of-fact way, and I looked at the reactions on my colleagues' faces. They were stunned listening to her, and soon after, one said to me: 'I am glad we came here. When you see these girls, you know that dreams can indeed come true.'

There was no need for any more scepticism. I could see change in front of my eyes. A girl from a relatively underprivileged background in Bhubaneshwar, with her family earning less than 7,000 rupees a month, could dare to dream. And along with her, the family was living the dream as well.

The real meaning of sport

Is sport about winning medals? Breaking records? Raising the bar? Or is it also about life lessons? Creating a better society and individuals? For the longest time, in India, the Olympic movement has been equated with a quadrennial sport competition. The world's greatest sport spectacle, which comes along every four years, and the nation's prestige is linked to the number of medals won. India doesn't have a record to boast about at the Olympics, and every Games is followed by the same refrain—of a country of a billion winning just a handful of medals. But then, are the Olympics just a sport competition? If that were the case, why use the word 'movement'? Do we say the FIFA World Cup movement or the ICC World Cup movement? We don't, and that's what differentiates the Olympic Games from every other sporting competition in the world. The Olympics are also about values, about life lessons, and a philosophy that calls for the creation of better societies. It was a delight to see each of these principles being implemented on the ground in the state schools in Odisha.

Each of the students enrolled as part of the Olympic Values Education Programme (OVEP) comes from an underprivileged background. Some are from slums, with little or no access to funds for education. Some did not have clean clothes to wear, and school was deemed a luxury. One of them actually used to stand outside the window, and see other students getting trained. It was only after a month that the teacher called her in, and asked if she wanted to join the school. Now, she was a regular and a class monitor. Speaking in English was an unimaginable proposition for almost all of them. To see them now engage with foreign visitors like Angelita in a language not their own was a wonderful surprise. Not only did they perform traditional Odia art forms with verve and confidence, but they went on to explain everything that they did to an audience of over 200 in perfect English.

These students were no longer insecure. No longer hesitant or underconfident. Rather, they were gradually getting ready to take on the world and make lives of their own. Something that had been unthinkable even a year or so earlier.

Let me go back to an incident that took place on April 3, 2023. It happened when a quiz was organised for some of the kids as part of the day's engagement. One of the questions asked was: 'Who is India's first-ever individual

Olympic gold medallist?' One of the youngest girls in the class raised her hand and, to everyone's surprise, said with utmost confidence: 'It is Abhinav Bindra, who won a gold at the 2008 Beijing Olympics.' When one of the staff members asked if she could spot Abhinav in the room, she looked straight at him, sitting in one corner of the room, and smiled. And Abhinav smiled back. A smile of immense satisfaction and joy, reminiscent of what I had seen on his face on the podium in Beijing all those years earlier. By doing what he was, Abhinav was making a huge difference. OVEP is helping to empower the kids of tomorrow and, in doing so, fighting centuries-old gender disparities that have plagued our society. By no means is it a finished product. Certainly not yet. But a start has been made, and a very strong foundation laid. And Odisha, with its keenness to embrace change, has made it possible.

Perhaps we should leave the last words to Angelita. 'India matters a great deal to the IOC,' she said. 'As a global movement, we need to make a difference to the maximum number of children we can reach out to. We will continue to back this initiative in Odisha. Go bigger, and spread it all across the state. How can you not when you see this kind of impact on the ground?'

Just then, a young girl walked up to her and said, again in perfect English: 'May I click a selfie with you, please?'

Very India. And as heart-warming as everything else seen that day.

Tailpiece

When the OVEP kids addressed the IOC session in Mumbai on October 15, 2023, we as a nation watched in awe and gratitude. This is what sport is all about.

A bunch of kids who have never attended an event like this, let alone address it. To even think what must be going through their minds is jaw dropping. And yet each of the kids were full of poise. When Bharti said 'Abhinav Bhaiya', I have never attended an event like this or spoken at an event like this', I was hoping she doesn't choke. In fact, was praying for her. She did not. Rather, she and the rest of the OVEP kids were all full of verve. Their passion was palpable. The pride was evident. In front of IOC President Thomas Bach and in the presence of Abhinav Bindra, they put Odisha and the OVEP programme at a very different pedestal at the IOC session in Mumbai.

And Abhinav, who always searches for real meanings through sport, must be hugely pleased. Having spoken to him almost daily, I am aware of the hard work he puts into the programme. Not just him. His entire team and the team in Odisha under the visionary leadership of CM Naveen Patnaik and his sports team led by R. Vineel

Krishna has transformed the lives of 200,000 kids with the Olympic Value Education Programme. At the end of the session when President Bach felicitated the kids and presented them with gifts, it was the most amazing moment of all. Kids, some of whom did not have access to education a year earlier, were being celebrated by the IOC President in the presence of Abhinav Bindra. Sport had given their lives a new meaning and the programme, which has now been embraced by the Reliance Foundation led by Mrs Nita Ambani and also by the Assam government led by Himanta Biswa Sarma, is already a success.

It was fitting that President Bach called the kids over for a photograph and seeing Abhinav stand a few feet away, called him into the frame. It was the perfect frame on what was a perfect day.

ODISHA AND HOCKEY

The Perfect Incredible India Story

'Odisha is the home of world hockey' is now a common refrain. With great infrastructure and facilities all across the state, fantastic sub-junior and junior programmes, proper talent scouting measures in place and the Naval Tata Hockey HPC in Bhubaneshwar as the pinnacle, not to forget the sponsorship of the Indian men's and women's hockey teams for a further 10 years, Odisha, under Shri Naveen Patnaik, has made giant strides in promoting hockey in the last one decade.

However, simply having world-class infrastructure is not enough. There are many examples of cities before us where great infrastructure was built for mega-events but which have subsequently been left unused and turned into white elephants. There has been no real connect between the city's inhabitants and sport. That's where

Odisha is unique. It is the home of world hockey because of the fans. Men, women and kids who love the sport and play it day in and day out all across the state have helped transform Odisha into the cradle of Indian hockey. Fans are the nerve centre of sport and help breathe life into it. They make the games come alive and make heroes out of the players.

Fan: the only constant loyalty in human life. In this age of information flow where space and time become irrelevant, one starts to become a sports fan at the age of five or six. And one turns into a committed follower even before touching double digits. For the next 70 to 80 years of his or her life, this is the only loyalty that endures.

You can have affairs, a broken marriage, changing tastes in food and clothing, and evolving views on politics. But a PR Sreejesh or Harmanpreet Singh fan aged five will remain one at 80. So much so that 50 years down the line, they won't take a backseat in arguing that Sreejesh, come what may, remains the greatest goalkeeper of all time.

This is one loyalty that will never be taken away from us. More powerful than nationalism, this is what makes modern sport the global marketers' dream. Brand Indian hockey, despite a World Cup loss, will always have the support of the loyal fans of Odisha. In fact, the loss has added to the possibility of redemption in Paris 2024, now that we know there is a tinge of mortality to this sort of immortality. Yes, India too, can lose and we need to back them all the way, for there is never any dearth of effort.

Sir Donald Bradman scored a duck in his last innings. Diego Maradona finished second-best to Germany with Andreas Brehme netting the decisive penalty in 1990. Roger Federer and Michael Phelps both lost on occasions. Usain Bolt too lost in the final individual race of his life. Sreejesh, in over 300 matches that he has played for India, has lost on many occasions. But just like the other greats mentioned here, he too will go down in history as one of the greatest. At least to his legion of fans in Odisha. And this community will forever remain a constant.

This was best evident in January 2023 when the Hockey World Cup finally started at the newly built Birsa Munda stadium. With 20,000 fans making the stadium home every night, it had a transformative effect on the sport. And the scenes were the same in Rourkela and Bhubaneshwar, making the World Cup a stupendous success.

The build-up would start more than three hours before an India game. Men and women with chants of *Bharat Mata ki Jai* and *Go India* would start to fill up the stands at the Birsa Munda Stadium or the refurbished Kalinga Stadium, depending on where India was playing.

Meanwhile, outside the stadium, it was all colour. Vendors doing up faces with the tricolour while others tried to sell their wares. Cricket fans like Sugumar, a feature at ICC tournaments, had landed up in India gear seeing the growing popularity of hockey and the quality of television broadcast. In sum, the Hockey World Cup was a high-quality spectacle that helped transform it into a mass-spectator sport.

While hockey in India has forever been a participatory sport, lack of proper marketing initiatives meant it could never compete with cricket as a spectator sport. The truth is cricket had all the glamour and spectator comforts, while hockey was a poor cousin, which failed to protect its players and draw in the crowds. The World Cup changed all that. Fan parks, which resembled the FIFA World Cup fan parks in Doha (2022), helped enrich the spectator experience and fan-engagement initiatives, which brought the players close to the supporters, helped transform the sport in India.

Media engagement with players ahead of the games, access to practice for the traveling media, entry to fan parks for the fans who had come from the world over, the World Cup was more like a carnival than just a hockey competition. And that's where the difference was made. It was no longer just a sport. It was a proper spectacle. Former Indian sports stars from across sports had been invited to Odisha for every India game, and each one of them shared photographs on social media adding to the occasion.

For the longest time, we have celebrated jugaad in hockey. We have celebrated players suffering. It is as if we take pride in writing or talking about players who live life in poverty, despite having played for India at the highest level. That they continue to struggle for a meaningful livelihood. The truth is it is shameful that they have to do so. It is disappointing we haven't been able to give them the kind of life they deserve. A sport that is rich will never let its own down. Cricket hasn't. Hockey will not. And that's where the World Cup was a breath of fresh air. It was great to see the 1975 World Cup-winning team congregate in Bhubaneshwar for a special felicitation. Most of these legends haven't met each other much in the last decade. In fact, it was great to see former players from the 1980 Moscow gold medal-winning team come together as well. It added to the occasion and encouraged many an aspiring youngster. The event, which was reported by the local press, pushed fans to buy tickets and make it to the stadiums. That every India game was sold out was the real story. There was a clamour for tickets that we haven't seen in hockey before and that's what had set the tournament apart from everything that had been staged in the past.

Can this be sustained in the days ahead? Can hockey become glamourous and crowd friendly? Odisha has shown the way. The state has helped built infrastructure, which is excellent, and made it accessible for the youth. Watching India play in Rourkela or Bhubaneshwar is now a craze and this should go a long way in putting backs on seats.

'The fandom in Odisha has no parallel in any part of the world,' said Sreejesh, one of the greatest to have played the sport. 'In Rourkela, it is just at a very different level. Players from across the world want to come and play in the Birsa Munda Stadium in front of packed crowds just to soak in the atmosphere. They will cheer you and encourage you and even if you don't get the desired result, they will stand by you in support. It is the same in Bhubaneshwar. Even after we had lost to New Zealand in the World Cup in January 2023, the kind of support we had received in Odisha was unrivalled. I can tell you that as a player I just love playing there because of these fans. They make you feel welcome to a very different level and it pushes you to perform better.

'When you play in front of packed stands, it automatically elevates your level of play. That's why it was so difficult during Covid. And that's why playing in Rourkela is so good and here I can speak on behalf of all the players. Also, the crowd in Rourkela really know their hockey. They know the new rules and when you make a good save, sometimes people just come and give you money and say they want to see more of such saves. That's when you know these fans are really special.'

Fan support for the sport is not restricted to international events or India games. Even when a junior tournament was held in Rourkela in mid-2023, there were 7000 to 8000 spectators in the stadium, which included a lot of young women and children. It was the perfect evening out with sport.

'When children see us play and do well, they too want to emulate us and play for India,' added Sreejesh. 'And when they see us play in front of them in a local setting, the feeling is: 'we can do this as well'. Playing in Rourkela has this impact on the local kids, many of who will perhaps take up the sport in the future. Kids in Rourkela don't just watch. They play as well. That's what is good about Odisha and that's why each one of us want to play there. It is our legacy and something we are deeply proud of.'

Rani Rampal, one of India's best women players of all time, echoes the same sentiment. 'We play for the flag,' said Rani. 'And when you have your own people cheering for you, it just adds to the occasion. It is like in front of these fans we can't lose. Ek alag hi josh aa jata hai. Aap jante ho there are thousands with you [It's a different kind of energy. You know there are thousands with you]. They are also playing with you. Passionate fan support makes a difference to every player.'

Speaking about the Tokyo performance where the Indian women's team led by Rani Rampal finished fourth, she put the fan support in perspective.

'Dekhiye medal medal hota hai. Medal na milna ek alag hi dukh tha. Par haan aap yeh keh sakte ho that humne dil jita in Tokyo [Look, a medal is a medal. Not winning one is a different sort of sorrow But yes, you can say we won hearts in Tokyo].'

While the disappointment will always remain, she was satisfied with the respect the team commanded back home in India. 'It was not until we came back to India that we realised what we achieved,' said Rani. 'The kind of respect we were shown on our return and the support we received made us feel we had done something worthwhile. And this was maximum in Odisha where we were honoured side by side with the men. Be it in the way the team was feted and the rewards that came our way, never were we discriminated because we had come fourth. It was a huge moment for us all and for the sport in India.'

For her as captain, it was a campaign to cherish. 'When I was young, I remember an occasion in 2004 when I went to the station in my native town to receive members of the Indian women's hockey team who had done very well at the Asia Cup in New Delhi and had won the gold medal,' said Rani. 'I was a kid then and there were four players from my town in the team. They were my heroes and I had carried garlands to the station to celebrate them. A lot of kids from the village were there and the euphoria among us all was something to be seen. That was when I had said to myself that if someday this same thing happens to me, my life will be fulfilled. And as luck would have it the very same thing happened after Tokyo. When we reached Odisha post the Olympics, the kind of euphoria we witnessed reminded me of my growing-up days.'

Odisha is not just about elite high-performance sport. And for the fans, it is not just passive consumption of the spectacle. In Rourkela, coaches like BJ Cariappa and Edgar Mascarenhas, who are both attached to the Panposh Sports Hostel, stay in the stadium residential complex, thus making it possible for the hostel students to have access to the best coaching talent. From the Birsa Munda Stadium to the Panposh Sports Hostel is a 10-minute drive, offering easy transportation and communication. Hostel students also get to practice in the world-class facility, exposure that can have a defining impact on their careers.

In fact, while the Birsa Munda Stadium is now the

central attraction in Rourkela and is like a jewel in the city's crown, the Panposh Sports Hostel is the hub where talent is honed. With all of it just a few kilometres apart, it has only added to the story of hockey in Odisha. Students who train at Panposh see the stadium regularly and, during events like the World Cup, are exposed to the best hockey action in the world. Seeing their heroes in front of them in the same city can work wonders and can only add to the glory of Panposh and Odisha, which has already produced 75 India internationals in the last decade and a half. If the Birsa Munda Stadium is the magnificent superstructure, Panposh is the foundation.

Kalu Charan Chowdhury and the Panposh story

As the flight touched down on the newly laid airstrip and the engines were turned off, the first thing that struck us was the silence. Unlike other airports, Rourkela is still one that works at its own pace and rhythm. It has this one flight coming in from Bhubaneshwar every afternoon, and the same flight travels back within an hour of landing in the city. It is more like a ferry service than a flight. Getting off the ATR via the ramp, the first thing you notice is the half-kilometre walk to the terminal. There aren't many buses plying to get the passengers transported and it is easily the best way to stretch your limbs after an hour of being cramped in the small flight seat. I actually loved the walk, which involves a couple of small jumps to get to the terminal, and while doing so, you can't but help admire the beauty around. On the one side are the hills, decorated further by the low-hanging monsoon clouds which add to the charm. On the other, peeking through from behind the green, is the imposing Birsa Munda Stadium, the jewel in Rourkela's crown.

With hardly four or five cars in the parking lot, there wasn't the usual wait as at most airports and we could get out of the terminal building in no time. Before visiting the Birsa Munda Stadium, the plan was to travel to the Sports Hostel in Panposh and speak to some of the residents there. The objective was to understand what hockey means to the locals in the Sundargarh area. It was just as we got going that we saw the street graffiti. Beautifully done, almost all of it is sports-themed, with hockey being the most dominant. As the Innova left the airport precinct and entered the bylanes on the way to Panposh, we saw what many had spoken to us about. It was a small patch of barren land and there was a small pond at the far end of it. A couple of cows were enjoying the afternoon breeze and some vegetable vendors were setting up their produce on one side of the road. In the middle of all this, there were six young boys playing hockey. As one of them scooped the ball, it was evident that they were regulars. He knew exactly where he wanted the scoop to land and the one receiving it did so seamlessly. At seven or eight, these boys are getting ready for a hockey future. This is the reality of Sundargarh—the hockey capital of India. In no other Indian city have I seen this. Cricket or football, yes, but not hockey. Rourkela is different, and that's what explains the crowds of over 20,000 each time India play at the Birsa Munda Stadium.

As the young kids disappeared from view, the excitement started to build, and we were getting restless. It was impossible to drive fast on the narrow roads, which are very similar to what we see in any suburban Indian town. Narrow and bumpy, with the monsoon having eaten into the top layer of the repair work, the only standout feature on the way was the Jagannath Temple. As the car crisscrossed the bylanes and made a sharp turn into yet another narrow alley, we first saw it. Two striking state-of-the-art hockey turfs in the middle of nowhere, with matches being played on both under the watchful eyes of Lazarus Barla, former India international, and BJ Cariappa, the coach who had taken over the national team ahead of the Pro League and after the sudden departure of Graham Reid. The pristine blue of the hockey turfs seemed a little out of place with all the dirty roads around. In all honesty, the hockey fields were the last thing one would have expected in the setting we were in. As the car slowed down, because two cows had decided to make the road theirs and some local women were busy chatting on one side on a lazy afternoon, we saw the first signage for the Panposh Sports Hostel. The boundary wall, yet again done up beautifully with mural art, celebrated almost every Indian star from Dhyan Chand to Deep Grace Ekka. You also have an MS Dhoni, a Dutee Chand and an Abhinav Bindra, making it a multi-sporting celebration of sorts.

Finally, we were at the Panposh Sports Hostel, which has produced 75 India internationals, 52 men and 23 women, in the last two decades. As we made our way in, a couple of young girls, who had just changed into their hockey uniforms, greeted us. They were getting ready to play a game against the veteran men's team and were slightly surprised to see a crew of five getting their cameras out to film.

That's when I was introduced to Kalu Charan Chowdhury, winner of the Biju Patnaik Award for his contribution to sport in 2021. Kalu Sir, as he is fondly known, has been part of Panposh from 1987 and was the first coach of Dilip Tirkey, current Hockey India President. As we settled down with a cup of tea each, Kalu Sir gave me my first reality check.

'Amit Rohidas is from this hostel,' he said. 'I am sure

you have seen him play for India. We have produced 75 India internationals and there are some who are in the national camp at the moment.' While the numbers were mind-blowing, I wasn't really interested in them to start with. I was interested in knowing more about Kalu Sir, for he is the quintessential Indian guru. Hardly celebrated beyond Odisha or accorded the recognition he deserves, his loyalty to the sport is what has kept him going.

'I have been here since 1987,' he said with a smile. 'What you are seeing now was just a barren grass field then. This was all TISCO [Tata Steel] land, and the sports hostel was to be built at a place 55 kilometres from here. The land had been identified and almost everything was final. That's when water came into the quarry, and the TISCO officials decided to give this piece of land to the State Sports Department and leave. With a grass field already here, the plan for the new hostel was abandoned and it was decided to convert this into a hostel for the boys.'

It was fate. Had the water not come into the quarry, the Rourkela story could have taken a very different direction. It did not and Tirkey first met Kalu Sir in the grass fields of Panposh in 1987. 'We travelled to the selection trials together,' said Kalu Sir, sipping on the elaichi tea we had been served with biscuits from a local store. 'Dilip had started out as a striker but at the time there were a number of very good players playing in the forward line. That's when he was tried out in the midfield but that too was packed. Finally, he was given a trial as a defender and he clicked. He kept getting better and you know the rest of the story.'

Just then, Lazarus, who mentors the hostel kids, shouted out instructions to one of the girls. Barla was himself playing for the veteran's team and also coaching. An imposing figure over six feet tall, Barla remains a Kalu Sir favourite even after all these years. 'He had serious talent,' said Sir, pointing towards Lazarus as he asked for another cup of tea with a wide smile. 'One time, as I came back to the camp, I was told that Lazarus had left for his village. He was very close to his mother, and was homesick. He just decided to leave without telling any one of us, I can tell you. I had to immediately travel to his village on my scooter and get hold of him. I told his mother that he had the potential to play for India and while his mother wasn't going anywhere, not being in the camp could spell disaster for his hockey career. She was convinced and I could get him back.'

It wasn't the only time that Lazarus fled the camp. 'He had left a second time when I was in Bhubaneshwar,' said Kalu Sir with a chuckle. 'He had one trouser, and during the monsoons, it hadn't dried in time after a wash. He left for his village because he did not have anything else to wear. For me, it was a lesson. While teaching them hockey, it was also important we kept an eye on what these talented but underprivileged kids needed. I got him back again, and took him to the government store and bought him some T-shirts and pants.

'He was one of the best I have seen. He had the height and the talent to play in any position. Between Dilip and Lazurus, the defence was well covered.'

The Lazarus story reminded me of what happened with the legendary Dhyan Chand in London in 1928. Remembering his first encounter with Dhyan Chand, Jaipal Singh Munda, India's captain at the 1928 Amsterdam Olympics, has written, 'He was humble. He had only one pair of trousers. I took him to Austin Reed on Regent Street. We went downstairs. Trousers galore were shown. 'Can I take them upstairs and see them in the sun?' That finished me. I told Shaukat the story. 'What else do you expect of a Lance Naik?' he laughed.'

The very same man was the greatest ever when he stepped on to the hockey pitch, and he eventually scored 14 of India's 29 goals in Amsterdam.

If it was Lazarus and Dilip in the 1990s, it is Amit Rohidas now. 'He is the fastest off the blocks during a short corner,' says Chowdhury. 'See him and you will know he is an all-round player.' A lot of the kids now model themselves on Amit and it is no surprise that a number of them consider him their hero. From the district of Sundargarh to becoming Vice-captain of the Indian team, he is a symbol of what Panposh can help a talented youngster achieve in world hockey.

Panposh got its first turf pitch in 1994, and it was exclusively set aside for the boys. There weren't too many girls then and it was manageable with one pitch, argued Chowdhury. With time, however, things changed. More and more girls started to come to the hostel and hockey turned into a real opportunity for social mobility. Playing well would guarantee a job and making it to the Indian team meant a good life. While there wasn't much money in the sport, it did lead to respectability for these kids and was a much better existence than one where a square meal a day is considered luxury.

'It was finally in 2012 that we had a second turf,' said Kalu Sir. 'Now the girls could also play and my aim was to produce the maximum number of players for the state and the country. These kids mostly come from poor backgrounds and it is important you get them interested in the game. They aren't too keen on theory so if you try telling them more about sports science and nutrition, they will lose interest. All they want to do is play. It is upon us to make the most of the talent available and at the same time mould their minds using the latest technology available.'

Panposh, in that sense, is the perfect harmony between the traditional and the modern. While on the one hand, we have the brand new turfs, installed just ahead of the Hockey World Cup in January 2023, on the other, the kids still come from backgrounds where they have little or no exposure. For them, it is all about skill and dribbling past a few players to show off how good they are. 'Modern hockey is very different,' says David John, Head of the Hockey HPC in Odisha. 'You can't hold the ball for too long. It is not the game anymore.'

'We can't tell the kids about sports science and technology and GPS,' said Kalu Sir. 'They won't understand. They haven't ever heard of these things. You have to understand where they are from. Most of these kids are from tribal backgrounds where hockey is a means to a better life. All they know is the hockey stick is a magic wand. The better they manage to use it, the better it is for them. The first struggle is to get two meals a day. Take care of the family. Then get a job. Their needs are very basic and you have to go down to their level to get the best out of them. Once they graduate from the hostel to the state and then the national camp, you can introduce sports science and a lot more.'

Now Panposh has everything it needs. It has two ultra-modern turfs, a very well-managed sports hostel with proper food and nutrition available to the students, and excellent coaches in Cariappa, Lazarus and Edgar Mascarenhas. Last year, in November, two teams, boys and girls, even travelled to Malaysia for an exposure trip.

'Things have changed dramatically in the last few years with the government making sports a huge priority,' said one of the senior administrators of the hostel. 'The two new turfs, which have been installed ahead of the World Cup means the students don't need to adjust when they move from here to Bhubaneshwar or to the national camp. They already have the exposure and are ready.'

'It was a conscious plan,' said R. Vineel Krishna, my co-author. 'We needed to ensure that our boys and girls don't need to make the shift from grass to turf pitches. Once your basic grooming is done, this shift is difficult and we have lost a lot of talented players in the process. The endeavour of the government has been to ensure we have the same turf pitches all across the state so that our players get the best exposure from the very start of their careers.'

But in all this, there is one constant. And that is Kalu Charan Chowdhury. Between 1987 and 2014, he was stationed in Panposh and helped stars like Tirkey, Lazarus, Ignace Tirkey and, now, Rohidas come through the ranks. He has seen 75 India internationals emerge from Panposh and find their feet in international hockey. Now a further 200 kids, 125 boys and 75 girls, are awaiting their tryst with hockey as they get ready in this cradle of talent.

'Covid meant we were not able to go out and scout,' said Kalu Sir. 'For two years, the supply line had dried up. We weren't able to meet the kids and get the best of them to Panposh. Now we have resumed doing so, and we are seeing more and more girls coming through the ranks.'

After serving for eight years in Bhubaneshwar between 2014 and 2022, he has been sent back to Panposh with an extension. And it is the right call, for that's where he belongs. A man of the soil, he has huge reserves of energy and will continue to serve and enrich Indian hockey for as long as he lives. Just as the boys and girls come out of the dressing room and greet him with a degree of reverence and respect, it is evident that he is as much a part of the Panposh story as the stars who have made it big. He is also what sport in Odisha stands for. Empowering talent irrespective of who you are, and in doing so, creating a new narrative for Indian sport. Kalu Sir is the story of Odisha hockey and, in a sense, the story of a new India that Odisha is trying to create and nurture.

Let's leave the last words to Tirkey, one of the greatest players to have come out of the state, 'Log hockey ke liye pagal hain [people are mad for hockey],' he said. 'People just love their hockey. They play from a very young age and watch every match that is played here. With all the facilities that are now available in the state, there is no debate Odisha is the new home of Indian Hockey. As president of Hockey India and on behalf of every fan, I must say this—the efforts of the last decade have helped transform the sport in India. We now have the best stadiums, the best sports science facilities, the best infrastructure and most importantly the best fans hockey could have hoped for. When you come to Odisha and you think of the Jagannath Temple, you also think of hockey. What more can we ask for? And things will only get better and better.'

UNLOCKING EXCELLENCE

Odisha's HPCs at Kalinga Stadium

Sports science

In the heart of the Kalinga Stadium, the sports science HPC stands as a beacon of progress and excellence for athletes far and wide. The Centre, a pioneering venture, stands as a testament to Odisha's enduring commitment to nurturing sporting talent. This institution embodies a philosophy that revolves around the athlete, offering a comprehensive sanctuary for those on the quest for sporting excellence. Its mission is unequivocal: to provide unwavering support, from identifying raw talent to providing expert guidance in training, rehabilitation, injury management, strength and conditioning, competition readiness, and bolstering mental fortitude, all underpinned by cutting-edge technology.

At its core lies an accomplished team of experts—physiotherapists, biomechanists, strength and conditioning specialists, sport scientists, sport medicine doctors, data analysts, nutritionists, sport psychologists, exercise physiologists and sport massage therapists, all united by a common goal: to cater to the diverse needs of Odisha's athletes and propel their growth and development. The Sport Science Centre is destined to be the nation's foremost hub for sport-science driven high-performance sport. This facility will not only contribute to the identification of budding talent; but also help sculpt training and rehabilitation programs that cater to the unique aspirations and needs of each athlete.

As athletes traverse this meticulously designed facility, they'll embark on a journey through specialized labs, each with a unique focus on different aspects of their development. These labs, as my team and I discovered, are at the heart of the Sport Science Centre, and they ensure that athletes receive the finest care and support tailored to their unique needs. This seamless navigation and continuous assessment within these labs cultivate their potential and drive them towards the pinnacle of excellence.

The first lab that you go into is the Postural Lab. It is a testament to the fusion of technological prowess and sports science. It holds the potential to revolutionize how athletes train and perform. This cutting-edge lab harnesses sensor-based technology for assessing balance and load distribution on the athlete's body. At its core, the Postural Lab is dedicated to perfecting an athlete's balance and overall posture, which are of paramount importance in the world of sports. By meticulously capturing data on a range of performance parameters such as static & dynamic stability, and posterior muscle chain imbalances, this lab becomes a treasure trove of insights that are indispensable for athletes striving to reach the pinnacle of their game.

Another cornerstone of athlete development is the Functional Lab. This lab focuses on perfecting an athlete's functional movements and sport-specific gestures. It relies on cutting-edge load sensor-based technology and the advanced 3D camera system, making it an invaluable resource in an athlete's training arsenal. Within the Functional Lab, athletes can refine their movements, ensuring they are not only precise but also tailored to the demands of their chosen sport. From enhancing strength and agility to boosting endurance, this lab provides a comprehensive array of vital metrics and insights. It's a place where athletes can fine-tune their skills, ultimately pushing the boundaries of their capabilities and overall performance.

In the Gait Lab, the future of athletic performance

and rehabilitation takes shape. With devices such as the Walker View, a compact gait analysis lab seamlessly integrated into a treadmill is at the heart of this innovative hub. This cutting-edge device delves into the intricacies of an athlete's gait and running style, yielding invaluable insights into the entire gait cycle. It scrutinizes every detail, from step length to trunk sway, joint rotation, and the centre of gravity amongst others, leaving no stone unturned. With this wealth of data in hand, coaches and therapists can craft training and rehabilitation programs with surgical precision, addressing each athlete's unique requirements. Moreover, the Gait Lab boasts an antigravity treadmill, a versatile tool to aid in both training and recovery.

In the ever-evolving world of sports, maintaining peak performance is a relentless endeavour. Athletes continually push their boundaries, seeking that extra edge that can set them apart. Enter cryotherapy, a revolutionary technique that has disrupted the sports arena. By subjecting the body to temperatures as low as -140 degrees for brief spells, cryotherapy has unlocked a realm of incredible benefits. It has become the ace up the sleeve for rapid recovery, reduction of muscle soreness, and overall performance enhancement. This frosty innovation sets off a chain reaction in the body, from quelling inflammation to unleashing endorphins, the body's natural painkillers. Cryotherapy is no longer just about feeling good; it's about performing at the pinnacle and bouncing back swiftly.

In high performance sport, where exacting standards and rigorous training regimens reign supreme, finding a means to unwind and recuperate is paramount. Sensory deprivation tanks, known as floatation therapy, have etched their place in the sporting landscape. These tanks provide athletes with a unique opportunity to escape the sensory bombardment of the external world and enter a realm of profound relaxation. Buoyed by salt-infused water, athletes effortlessly float, shedding the relentless pull of gravity. In this serene cocoon of silence and darkness, minds gain clarity, and bodies embark on a healing journey. The benefits are myriad—from stress and anxiety reduction to the alleviation of muscular tension and support for injury recovery. It's akin to hitting a reset button for both body and mind, offering athletes the mental and physical rejuvenation essential for achieving peak performance.

Within the heart of the cutting-edge physiology lab, innovation meets precision. The linchpin of the physiology lab is the portable metabolic measurement system, which allows the experts to delve deep into the intricacies of oxygen uptake and metabolic responses during exercise. Whether assessing an athlete's VO2 max to fine-tune their training regimen or monitoring the metabolic health of recovering athletes, the device provides data accuracy and real-time insights. But it's not just about data; it's about performance optimization. That's where the range of ergometers and treadmills comes into play. These precision instruments are engineered to push athletes to their limits while maintaining unparalleled control and accuracy. Whether it's cycling ergometry or treadmill testing, the equipment ensures that every stride, every pedal, is measured with utmost precision. It's the synergy of technology and physiology, where the metabolic measurement systems and the ergometers join forces, providing athletes and experts alike the tools they need to unlock new levels of human performance.

Speaking on this aspect, Dr Digpal Ranawat, Head of the HPC states, 'Our commitment to pushing boundaries doesn't end there. Within our physiology lab, we've incorporated an altitude training chamber that takes performance enhancement to new heights—literally. Athletes know that elevation can be a game-changer, and our chamber allows them to experience the benefits of high-altitude training without leaving the ground. Whether it's for endurance athletes seeking to boost their red blood cell count or sprinters looking to fine-tune their oxygen utilization, our altitude chamber offers a controlled environment for tailored altitude training programs. It's where science and sport converge, where athletes come to adapt, and where limits are redefined.'

He went on to add, 'Inclusivity and innovation are at the core of our sporting ethos, which brings us to the Para-Athlete Performance Lab. This is a space dedicated to the para-athletes in the ecosystem. Within this cutting-edge facility, we've installed the largest treadmill in the country, designed not only for able-bodied athletes but also with the comfort and adaptability required for wheelchair athletes. It's a testament to our commitment to levelling the playing field and providing a training environment that caters to every athlete's unique needs. But that's not all; the lab is equipped with specialized Wheelchair and Arm ergometers, ensuring that the para-athletes have access to the tools they need to excel in their chosen disciplines. It's a place where differences are celebrated, where determination knows no bounds, and where we're helping athletes of all abilities reach their full potential.

Picture a sophisticated system of high-speed cameras, force plates, and powerful real-time assessment software—all orchestrated to elevate an athlete's performance to astonishing heights. In this domain, every movement, every action, is subjected to meticulous scrutiny. The biomechanical assessment in sports is akin to a magnifying glass for athletes. It dissects their every move, analysing the mechanics of their performance. Imagine a hockey athlete refining their swing or a sprinter optimizing their stride length using real-time feedback accurate to the last degree. That's the magic of biomechanics. Here, athletes receive personalized insights, honing their movements to perfection and optimizing their techniques for the demands of their specific sport. It's a precision tool that leaves no room for guesswork, ensuring that every motion an athlete makes is nothing short of excellence.'

The sports science HPC is also focussed on the mental health of athletes. In sports where physical prowess often takes centre stage, we recognize that mental fortitude is equally vital. The Mind Lab is a sanctuary for our athletes to not only hone their cognitive skills but also to confront the unique stresses and challenges that accompany their athletic journey. In this safe haven, cutting-edge devices stand ready to sharpen their mental acuity, while a team of dedicated sport psychologists provides guidance and mentorship. Here, athletes learn to navigate the intense pressures of their sport, build resilience in the face of adversity, and cultivate the winning mindset that sets champions apart. The Mind Lab is more than a training ground; it's a place where athletes become not only physically strong but mentally invincible.

The path to glory often encounters unexpected hurdles—injuries. While every effort is made to minimize their occurrence, their inevitability cannot be denied. This is where the technology offered at the Rehabilitation Lab steps in. Led by therapies like shockwave therapy, TECAR therapy, high-power laser treatments, and electrotherapy, athletes are offered the best of care! These devices assist in pain management by extinguishing the root cause and igniting the flames of healing. This technology helps in soothing fatigued muscles, gently easing away their weariness. These devices also work their magic on deep tissues, expediting the body's natural healing mechanisms. These non-invasive marvels offer athletes a holistic approach to pain management, swelling reduction, and a speedy return to peak performance.

The Sport Science Centre at Kalinga Stadium doesn't just represent innovation; it embodies a transformative force. This facility is poised to have a profound impact on the Odisha Sport Ecosystem, nurturing talent and creating champions. By providing athletes with the finest expertise, personalized training, and the power of data-driven insights, it will pave the way for dreams to be realized and records to be shattered. The Sport Science Centre isn't merely a facility; it's a symbol of Odisha's commitment to sporting excellence. As the Sport Science Centre begins operations, the core focus will be on shaping futures and creating a lasting legacy of sporting achievement. The impact of this endeavour will ripple far beyond the boundaries of Odisha, inspiring generations to come and setting new benchmarks for excellence in sports.

Trying it out

'You must experience it yourself,' said Abhinav as I spoke to him on the morning of the visit. 'There is nothing to be scared of and we do it on a daily basis. Unless you experience it first-hand you won't know what all I am speaking about,' he said. Within moments, Dr Digpal called and reiterated the same. 'We have informed the team at the Kalinga Stadium that you all will be visiting. If you want to write about it check out every facility and try for yourself. Then you can call me with any questions you have,' he said.

I liked the transparency. That's what excellence is all about. When you know your work well, it automatically gives you the confidence to strive for excellence and that's what Dr Digpal and his team do on a daily basis at the Sports Science HPC. And yes, we did try the cryo. Two of my colleagues, Trisha Ghosal and Sharmistha Gooptu, tried the experience and were hugely appreciative of it. As they went in and the machine completely enveloped them, I was keeping time. The men in charge informed me that they had set the timer at two minutes instead of three because they were both amateurs and that way would love the experience. Every instruction was given in advance and the attention to detail is what stood out for me. Most young athletes who try out these machines for the first time have little or no idea what they are getting into. Some of them haven't ever heard of cryo, let alone experienced it. It is one thing to just tell them to do it but a completely different thing to take them into confidence and explain why they are being asked to use the therapy.

It was after a couple of hours that Sharmistha informed me of feeling completely relaxed and sleepy. That's what the cryo does. It helps in athletes' recovery and works on the fatigue to get them ready for another gruelling encounter the very next day. HS Prannoy, one of India's best badminton players, has multiple times emphasised the importance of recovery. 'In badminton, you have to play matches on a daily basis in most competitions. And some of these matches can go on for as long as an hour and a half. The body needs time to recover. If you don't have the time, you are sure to feel tight and stiff when you go on to court the next day. That's where the cryo makes a huge difference. In fact, the fact that I am able to perform at this level is largely because of the improvement in sports science,' said Prannoy.

Rohan Bopanna, who created a world record by making the US Open final at 43 years and six months, also

The athletes march past is always a telling nationalist moment.

A transformed Kalinga Stadium is now one of the best in the country.

Winning in front of a packed home crowd is the greatest joy of all.

Odisha is now defined by its world class infrastructure.
But the journey hasn't always been easy.

Recognition is always inspiration.

Hon CM Shri Naveen Patnaik with Oly the turtle-mascot of the 2023 Hockey World Cup.

Even during Covid, Odisha under Shri Naveen Patnaik consistently backed the growth of Indian hockey.

Swimming is one of Odisha's priority sports and the state has already organised multiple competitions.

The joy on the faces of the children is the story.

Sunil Chhetri has time and again spoken about the support he has received from fans in Bhubaneshwar.

The FIFA U-17 Women's World Cup was a spectacular success.

It has always been about multi-sport for the Hon. Chief Minister.
Here Shri Naveen Patnaik is with the Indian U-17 women's football team.

Lord Sebastian Coe was left hugely impressed with the way Odisha stood up to the challenge of organising the Asian Athletic Championships.

Under lights the Birsa Munda Stadium is an architectural marvel.

An aerial view of the Kalinga Stadium- the venue for the final.

Each time the Indians ran out in the newly established Birsa Munda Stadium in January 2023, it was a sight to behold. The packed crowd was delirious.

The Hon. CM has always believed in the power of sport. Having played hockey as a young man, the sport has always had a special place for him.

Recognition from the Guiness Book of Records for the Birsa Munda stadium.

Recognition for work done in promoting sport. The presence of the iconic Sunil Gavaskar seen presenting the trophy to the Hon CM adds to the moment.

Once a player, always a player.

The Khelo India University Games made a real impact on the Indian sporting eco-system. Here, former Sports Minister, Government of India, Shri Kiren Rijiju is seen with Hon. CM Shri Naveen Patnaik.

The Super Cup at its home. It is now the Kalinga Super Cup. Continuity is the name of the game.

Time and again Abhinav Bindra has spoken about the support he has received from Odisha and the CM Shri Naveen Patnaik.

OVEP kids with Director of the Olympic Foundation for Culture and Heritage, Angelita Teo.

With Frederique Jamolli,
Head of International Cultural Affairs for the IOC.

IOC representatives and Abhinav Bindra with the mixed gender teams, which is the standout feature of the programme.

While the girls started with a sense of apprehension, some of them are now better than the boys and are captains of their respective teams.

The confidence and passion is what stood out in each of these kids.

The competition is intense. Mixed gender kho kho.

OVEP Kids with a very content Hon. CM Shri Naveen Patnaik.

Even the IOC President Thomas Bach was left profoundly impressed.

OVEP kids at the IOC session in Mumbai in October 2023.

The Indian hockey team has always felt at home in Odisha.
Skipper Harmanpreet Singh has said so time and again in his interactions.

These kids are the future. A future of hope and optimism.

Celebration time.

People from all age groups love their hockey in Odisha.
Every game played is packed.

Playing in front of packed home crowds have also helped the Indian team in the last few years. The rankings reflect that.

Days before the competition started, every India match was a sell out. That's what stands out about hockey and Rourkela.

Under lights, it is just a spectacular sight.

Each time India scores, the roar is defeaning.

The dream is to see this sight in Paris 2024.

Winning is a habit and that's what Odisha has tried to help the Indian team inculcate.

The best hockey stadium in the world.

The Panposh Hostel has forever been a cradle to hone talent.

The state of the art sports science center helps in athlete rehab and recovery.

The newly opened state of the art Sports Science Centre has every modern equipment that athletes might need.

With high-quality infrastructure at hand, every team has loved to visit and play in Odisha.

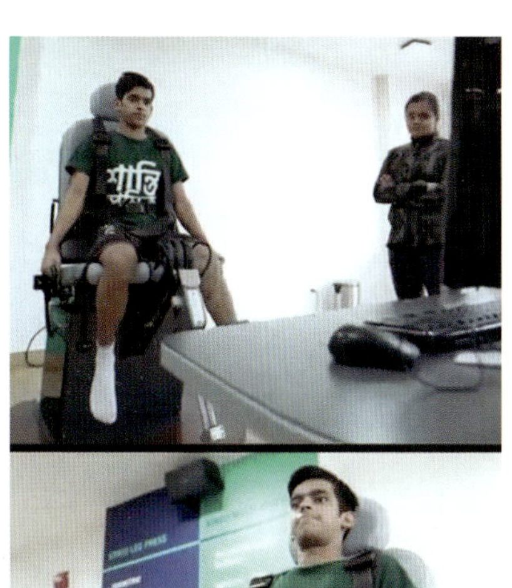

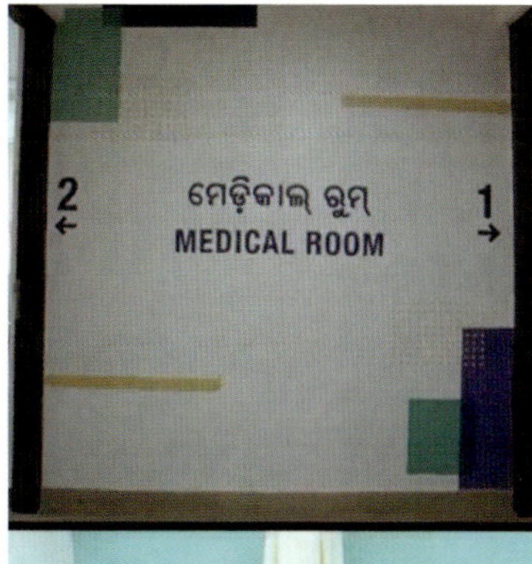

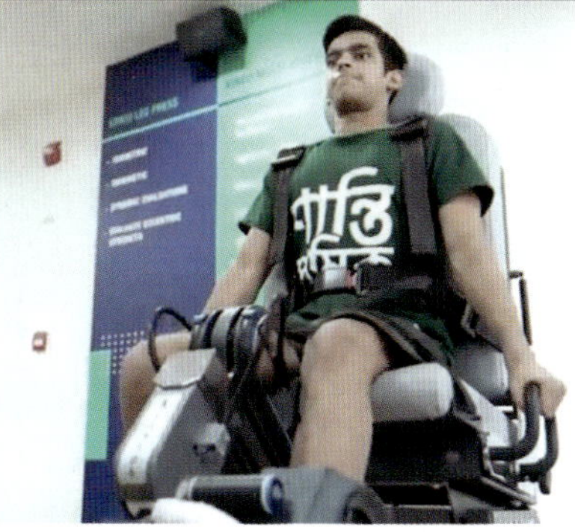

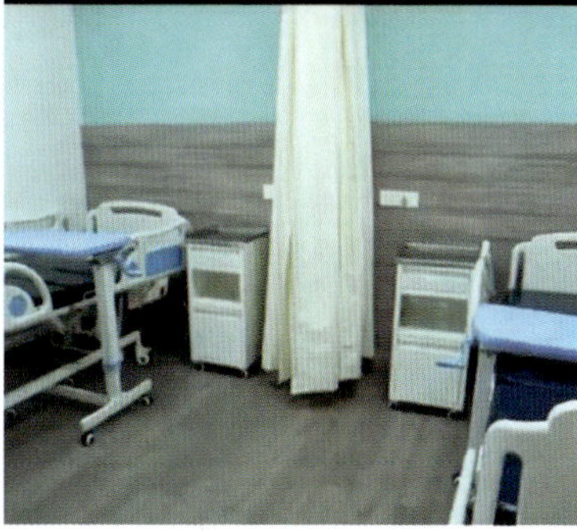

Recovery and rehab are integral to success.

Jhilli Dalabehera is one of the many young stars coming out of Odisha and is expected to make it big in weightlifting.

India lacked facilities like these forcing athletes to go outside the country to train.

Athletes recovery after a gruelling race is as important as the preparation and that's what is now part of the routine in Odisha.

The state of the art gymnastics facility is a new addition to the list of HPCs.

With such infrastructure spread across the state, almost every city or town now has its own unique space in the sports landscape and offers much needed encouragement for aspiring athletes.

With Mirabai Chanu winning the Olympic medal in Tokyo, young lifters across Odisha now believe in the Olympic dream and the HPC is only going to help them realise their ambition.

Such facilities will surely help fulfil the dream of a multi sport India in the years to come.

Odisha has made sure hockey is a source of empowerment for every girl playing the sport.

Rahul Bose has made a telling impact on Rugby India.

The story of women's rugby is one of the best stories of talent meeting opportunity.

Multiple players in the national team are from Odisha.

The shooting HPC will add to a sport that is already on an upswing in India.

Every stadium in Odisha now is of international standard

HOCKEY

These women speak a story of empowerment.

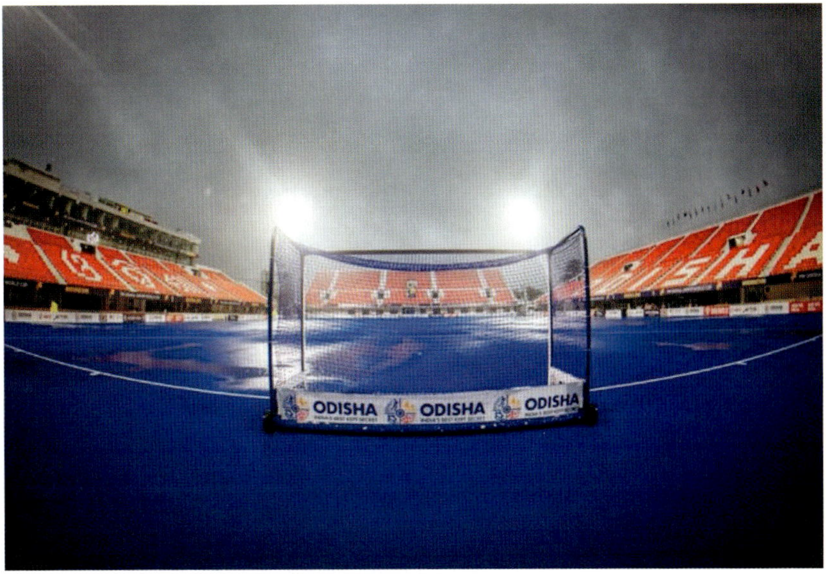
ODISHA
ODISHA
ODISHA

MAJOR DHYAN CHAND

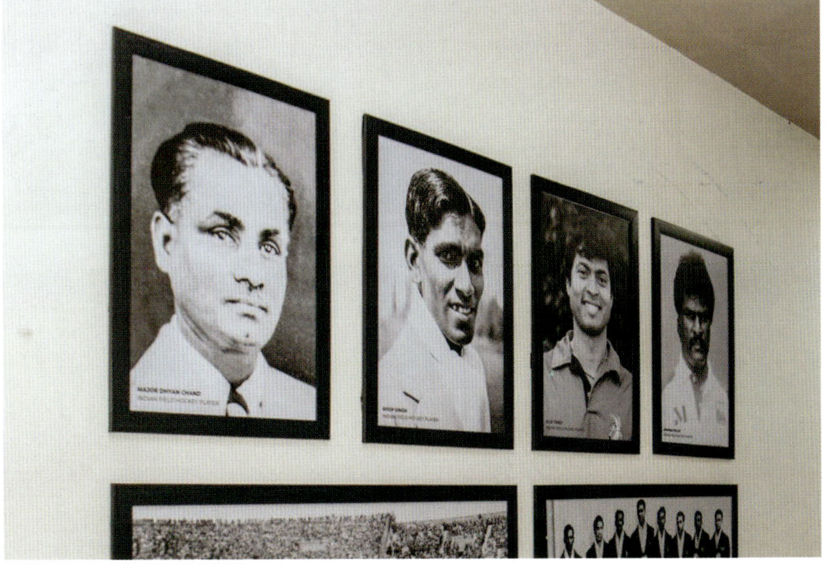

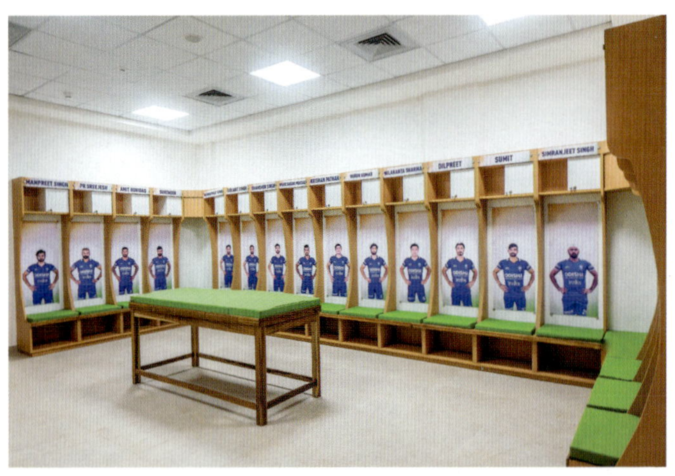
MANPREET SINGH
PR SREEJESH
AMIT ROHIDAS
NILAKANTA SHARMA
DILPREET
SUMIT
SIMRANJEET SINGH

High quality infrastructure has the potential to transform Indian sport.

From grassroot to high performance, everything is taken care of.

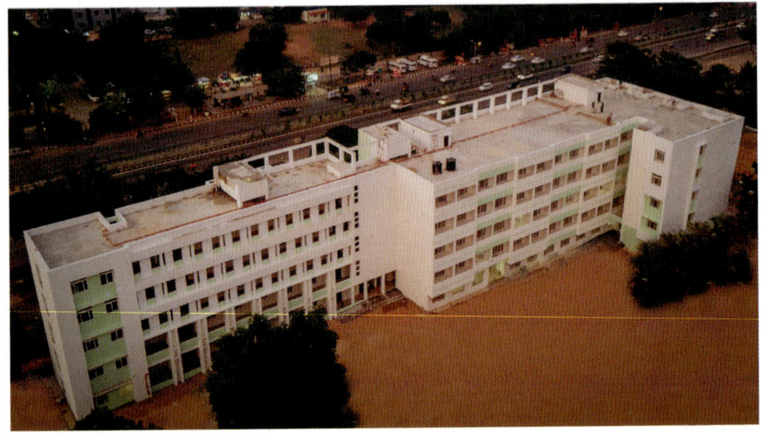

The photograph says it all.

Breeding ground of champions.

Such stadiums will always encourage kids to play the sport.

Multi sport with equal emphasis is the story.

Kishore Jena is the newest star on the block.

Shri VK Pandian with Mr. Arsene Wenger and AIFF President Shri Kalyan Chaubey.

Aerial view of the precinct that is fast becoming the hub of Indian sport.

Now Odisha is home to the AIFF-FIFA Talent Academy as well, which was inaugurated in the presence of the legendary Arsene Wenger.

The AIFF Fifa talent academy has the potential to make a real difference to Indian football and yet again Odisha could be the new home for the sport.

Pictures Speak a Million Words

Odisha and Tata Steel sign MOU to establish HPC's for Archery and Sports Climbing. Shri Naveen Patnaik with Shri Chanakya Chaudhary, Vice President Corporate Services, Tata Steel.

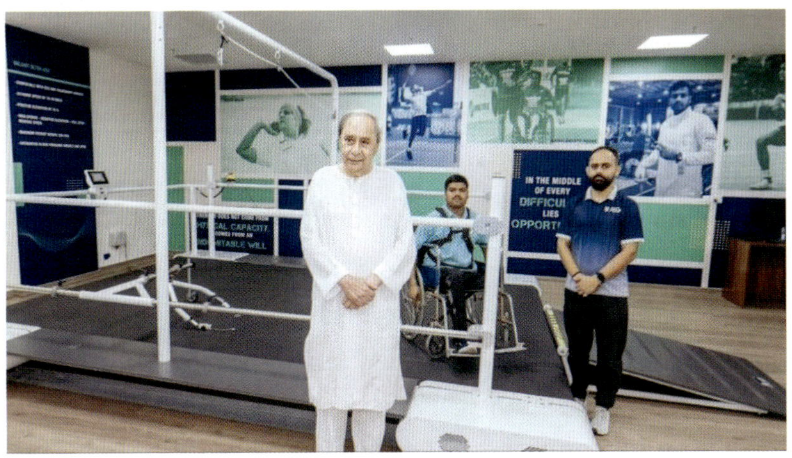

Shri Naveen Patnaik at the newly established Sports Science Center.

alluded to how his career has been resurrected thanks to sports science. 'I was able to work out the whole recovery plan with my team. They get me ready for the next day and are not often celebrated for the work they do. You need to be at your best every single day in elite high-performance sport and that's where sports science has become critical,' said Bopanna.

As we were in the closing stages of our visit to the HPC, a very young athlete of 16 came in. She looked scared and vulnerable. 'Maine kabhi yeh sab machine nahi dekhi hai [I've never seen all these machines before],' she said and the words were hardly audible. Her coaches and trainers had asked her to do a few tests and now it was on the HPC team to make her feel comfortable. I was looking at the whole thing with a lot of interest. As the lady doctor in charge started to fit the machines, she started to simultaneously engage the athlete into a conversation about her family and what brought her to athletics. And as the young girl was describing how much it means to her parents that she is now into sport, the doctor had finished one of her tests. It was seamless. And as she informed the athlete that the test was complete, there was a look of complete amazement on her face. She did not even feel it and was elated. With a huge smile on her face, she gave the doctor a hug. The doctor looked slightly embarrassed because I was looking on.

But at that one instant, I had experienced the best of sport. The HPC is a symbol of excellence with the best of global treatments and methods. It employs the best equipped personnel to take care of the athletes. And here was a young girl who was just cutting her teeth into sport. It was the best mesh of the conventional and the modern. The best example of how incredible India is and how much talent this country has. And now thanks to the Government of Odisha, a section of the talent is being harnessed. For a long time, talent did not meet opportunity. Now it's happening and that's what leaves me with a sense of hope and optimism for India's sporting future with Odisha leading the way.

Gymnastics

Everything in the Kalinga Stadium precinct is within walking distance. And it was within minutes that we were at the newly opened Gymnastics High Performance HPC in partnership with the ArcelorMittal Nippon Steel (AM/NS) having completed our ethnography at the Sports Science Centre.

Interestingly, the Asian Games Gymnastic trials had just concluded at the newly established High Performance Centre and Dipa Karmakar, who was making a comeback after a 21-month ban, was the cynosure of all attention.

Dipa had performed well and had topped the trials and was understandably elated at a possible opportunity of representing India at Hangzhou. That things did not go to plan for her and her name was omitted at the last minute is a different story, but it doesn't take away from the fact that she was delighted with the facility and said as much in a conversation with me.

Soon after the event was over, did we have a chat. 'I am very happy to be on the mat again. Coming back is like getting my life back,' she said. While she wasn't completely injury free and was still not at her best, it was evident that Dipa had done enough to ignite interest of a lot of fans who had all come to watch her. 'This is a fantastic facility. When I saw it for the first time, I couldn't believe my own country now has a facility of this standard and scale. Every detail has been looked into and everything that a gymnast needs is at hand. On behalf of everyone who plays the sport I need to thank the Government of Odisha for setting this up,' she said. Her coach, Bisheshwar Nandi, a Dronacharya awardee, went a step further. 'I have been in coaching for decades now,' he said. 'And I can tell you with complete certainty that in India we do not have a facility of this quality and scale. Everything here is world class. And with access to a recovery facility and the sports science facility, every athlete will want to come and train here.'

Ashok Mishra, Head Coach of the Indian Gymnastics team, is ecstatic with the facility. Sitting in his first-floor office overlooking the training going on through the glass windows, he said, 'This is a matter of great pride for the sport that we now have a facility of this standard. Except in Delhi there is nothing like this in the country and this is as good if not better. Every detail has been looked into and what makes this HPC special is its proximity to all the other HPCs and especially the Sports Science HPC. A number of athletes are always here training in these facilities and they keep meeting each other. Such things rub off and makes for great camaraderie. If you see someone else trying to excel, you feel the same urge to push the bar,' he said.

I was immediately reminded of what Viswanathan Anand said about the golden generation of Indian chess, yet another sport that Odisha has started to actively get into. Speaking to me in Kolkata during the Tata Steel Chess in September 2023, Anand had said, 'I will say they are all rivals and are extremely competitive and at the same time are very good friends. Now that one is past 2700 in the ratings you will see all of them going for 2700. If one has done well, all of the others will want to do well. I can tell you from experience it always happens. Boris Gelfand who is now coaching the boys and I had a similar experience. If one of us tried a new opening, the other had to get it for that's how you stay competitive. That's what is happening with this group. But I have also asked myself that if they are such close friends where is the rivalry! You try to see the signs and always know that there is intense rivalry but there is also great friendship.'

He went on to add, 'I am sure there is rivalry but at the same time there is great friendship. They have all grown up playing the junior circuit, their parents have sat outside when the players are playing and they are all very good friends which is a great thing. And from personal example I can tell you some of my most intense rivals are now some of my best friends. It is because we can't discuss these things with anyone else and that sort of works for the friendships.'

Sport can be a very isolating experience at times and practicing day in and out away from public glare is never easy. That's where friendships are forged and make a difference. These HPCs which are all in touching distance of each other make for such possibilities. To see a Rani Rampal coaching young kids in the hockey HPC is something a young gymnast will surely be enthused about. To hear from Rani, whichever sport you play, is always an incentive. It is no longer about one centre of excellence. Rather, Odisha has now been able to create a number of enclaves of excellence for Indian sport with each feeding off the other.

Yet again the Gymnastics HPC isn't a standalone centre. The supply line too has been adequately taken care of and hundreds of young kids are now getting attracted to the sport as a result. A feeder centre has been created in Puri and I was amazed to see the excitement among the kids during my visit late afternoon on July 16, 2023.

Nineteen acres of land in the heart of Puri. Literally seven minutes from the beach. And as you enter the Jagannath Cricket Stadium, which is a composite facility for sport with gymnastics being the other sport in the complex, you are transported to any other facility in the West. Clean with state-of-the-art facilities, the gymnastics facility trains kids between the ages of six and fourteen. And in the two hours that I was there, a couple of kids really caught my eye with the skill on show. By the time it was 6 p.m. and the sun was just about to set, we decided to take a break from work and venture on to the beach. While we did so, the kids, however, were working hard in training. Under the watchful eyes of the coaches, this centre will act as the perfect supply chain for the HPC in Bhubaneshwar.

Yet again, what stands out about this centre is the attention to detail. It is part of a larger sports enclave of excellence and the trainees have access to every form of expertise at hand. And that it is in Puri means local talent don't necessarily have to travel to Bhubaneshwar to make a career in sport. It is this decentralisation that is a standout feature of the Odisha model of sports governance. 'We needed to connect the entire state and not just restrict ourselves to Bhubaneshwar. Just like we constructed the Birsa Munda Stadium in Rourkela to harness local talent, the idea to build this stadium complex in Puri was to ensure every local kid has access to facilities and infrastructure and we don't lose out on talent. No one should have to give up sport because there are no opportunities. Our job is to make the best facilities available to all our citizens and create the ground for talent to prosper,' said my co-author, when I met him in July 2023 to try and understand the vision of the Chief Minister.

What the Puri infrastructure also does is it sets up the possibility of sports tourism in the amazingly popular tourist town. The Blue Flag beach in Puri, may I say, is one of the best in the country. With a little more marketing, it is as good as Chennai or even the Bondi in Sydney. The first thing that stands out about the beach is how clean it is. No garbage, no littering, beautifully done up with benches and flags and the breeze that will give the best feel of nature, it is the perfect evening in every sense. And that's when you see the Blue Crab and Nimantran, two excellent restaurants run by the Odisha Tourism Development Corporation. Sitting in one of the armchairs of the Blue Crab sipping a virgin mojito and tasting some delectable prawns, it isn't too far away from what we call bliss.

'We have plans of integrating sports tourism as part of the Blue Flag beach,' says Lenin Mohanty, Chairman of OTDC. 'There is real scope here to do adventure sports also. We have families visiting and we want all of them to do some form of physical activity when here.'

A very hands-on man, he has a dream of making the Blue Flag beach one of India's most-loved tourist destinations. 'Sport is something we in Odisha take a lot of pride in,' says Mohanty. 'Our honourable Chief Minister has helped us become the sports hub of India. It is only natural we integrate sports with tourism and offer visitors a package that they won't get anywhere else.'

Sports like beach volleyball, which have huge appeal in the West and in the Olympics, should indeed be promoted in Puri. A mix of sport, food, tourism and culture, which includes a must-visit to the famous Jagannath temple, could give Puri an edge that no other city in India can match.

Weightlifting

At the time we visited this HPC, a lot of activity was going on with a fairly large delegation from Kerala visiting the centre to get first-hand experience. What this meant was the administrators weren't really with us always and it allowed us an opportunity to explore things on our own. Nothing had been decked up. Rather, it was all organic and the ground floor hall was buzzing with activity. With lifters, men and women, from across age groups trying to perfect the art under the watchful eyes of the Hungarian coach, you could just sense the intensity. The clangs of the metal being dropped on the floor and the cacophony of noise everywhere, the place was buzzing. 'There is a lot of talent. But what we need to do is hone that talent and make sure they don't overdo things. Weightlifting is a sport in which there is always the chance of an injury. And once you are injured, it could impact your career unless you get into a proper recovery process. These students are always keen to practice and often end up overdoing things. So, while I focus on technique and performance, I am also conscious in ensuring they remain fit and healthy,' said the coach.

Operational since February 2019, the Weightlifting HPC is managed by the Anil Kumble-promoted TENVIC Sports and has been delivering significant sporting results since within a year of its foundation. 'Fourteen weightlifters who trained at the Centre won 12 golds and five silvers at the State Weightlifting Championship held in September 2019. In February 2020, Kumbheswar

Mallik from the HPC won a bronze in the 55 kgs category at the Khelo India University Games,' states the Tenvic website.

It goes on to add, 'While TENVIC Sports focuses on holistic and scientific training for a weightlifter to achieve peak performance in the sport, we also ensure that the young athletes do not compromise on academic excellence. The athletes continued to pursue their education through online classes during the period of the pandemic. TENVIC Sports supplements the formal education curriculum with classroom learning in the HPC bubble. The teachers hold classes on a variety of subjects that cover academic courses like mathematics, computer science and English, but also others that complement academics and sports—communication, psychology and preparing for competitive exams, for instance.'

By the time we had finished with speaking to the coaches and some of the athletes on the ground floor, the head of the facility, Colonel Rajesh Sharma had invited us for a cup of tea to his office a floor above. He had just finished with the Kerala delegation and finally had a breather. On entering his office, the first thing that struck us was the television, which was connected to the internet and livestreaming of the Commonwealth Weightlifting Championship from Noida. Seeing my gaze, the Colonel started off on Jyoshna Sabar who had won the best youth weightlifter award at the Commonwealth Championships in the 40 kgs category, her second major triumph after winning the nationals in Tamil Nadu. 'Jyoshna comes from a remote village. When we learnt of her talent, we got her to the HPC and now she is one of the most promising weightlifters in India. This is what the centre stands for. Giving the youth opportunities they did not have in the past.'

Ravi Kumar, former Indian weightlifting great, is very upbeat about Jyoshna. Soon after she had won her first international medal, Ravi had commented, 'It's an incredibly proud moment for all of us. This is her first international competition and she has won a medal at her first attempt. It reminded me of my own career when I had won a silver in 2007,' Ravi had said. Coaching Joshna since March 2022, at the Odisha HPC, he predicts a bright future for the young 14-year-old.

Sabar is just one among many Odisha lifters who have started to dominate the national scene. And that's what the future is all about—Odisha as a leading sports hub. Excelling in multiple sports, the state is now on the cusp of a sporting revolution of sorts with the HPCs leading the way.

Last words: The story has just begun

With swimming and tennis added to the existing lot of HPCs, the next five years could completely transform the sports landscape in the state. While we have already started to see Odisha athletes winning medals in national and international competitions, the best, clearly, is yet to come.

To go back to the words of the Chief Minister, 'Our model of partnership and high-performance centres have drawn national attention. It is an endorsement of our vision, investment and efforts in sports. This is an opportunity for each one of us to work together with heightened commitment to take sports to greater heights'.

ODISHA'S *CHAK DE* GIRLS

'It was a few weeks after I had taken charge as High Performance Director of the Hockey HPC in Bhubaneshwar,' said David John, his voice rising with every sentence. 'I had travelled to Delhi to see a tournament where our girls were playing a team from SAI. That's where I spotted this girl who was playing for SAI. When I found out that she was Odia, I inquired why she wasn't playing for us. I was told she wasn't part of the academy and was a product of the SAI Centre in Sundargarh. I just felt she needed to play for us and requested that she be selected for the state team in the National Games. She did well and within a few months was fast tracked into the Junior National Programme and was part of the team that travelled to Japan for the Asia Cup. It was her goal that separated India and Japan in the final and, overnight, Sunelita Toppo had found her feet in international sport.'

One of the most experienced coaches and High Performance Directors in the world, John has been around long enough to separate the best from the rest. 'She is special,' said John. 'Trust me when I say this to you. Within months of the Junior Asia Cup, she was taken into the senior programme and is now part of the senior women's national team and could well be that she is in Paris in 2024 to play the Olympics. And she is just 16.'

The Toppo story is the perfect one of talent meeting opportunity. Eighteen months ago, she was playing around with teenage cohorts in the Kukuda village of Sundargarh. The village is 303 kms from Bhubaneshwar and 65 kms east of the district headquarters in Sundargarh.

In every sense, the village is not your normal choice to produce a world beating athlete. Like most kids in the village play hockey as a pastime, Sunelita also played hockey since she was 8 years old. However, it was never with an aim to play the sport professionally. Born into underprivilege and struggle, hockey was a kind of stress buster for the young Sunelita. Literally for every kid in her area, the hockey stick is a symbol of empowerment and joy. That's when they forget the struggle and the strife and just find joy and happiness. It was the same for her when she first played the sport.

Her first love, however, was athletics. If you see

her build you will know why. She is lean and athletic and track and field came naturally to her. With limited facilities around for hockey in her village, athletics was a natural option. 'I spoke to her coach Beas Remi in Sundargarh and he said he spotted her in an athletics competition,' said John. 'He would go to these athletics meets and in one of them he had seen Sunelita. Finding her energetic and sporty, he asked her if she wanted to try her hand at hockey. She did and that was a kind of Eureka moment for Indian women's hockey.'

It was almost destined to happen. From being spotted in an athletics meet to being brought into the SAI centre, the Sunelita journey has an element of amazement attached to it. It was her coach who first said to her what sport could do for her in the years ahead. If she played hockey well, she could be a part of the Indian set up and travel around the world. It was a life of prestige and affluence and a means to come out of underprivilege. Hockey was her ticket to mobility and Sunelita had no reason to shy away from the opportunity.

Listening to the story I was taken back to a conversation I had with a young Sakshee Malik in Rio soon after she had won India's first medal at the 2016 Olympics. PV Sindhu had added a second medal to the tally a few days later. Sakshee, innocent as she was, had come to the Main Press Centre soon after the medal ceremony to interact with the Indian media. 'I was always fascinated by aeroplanes,' she had said. 'Each time I spotted a plane over my village I felt excited and wondered if I could ever get into one. Wrestling offered me an opportunity to do so. I was told that if I did well, the government would put me on an aeroplane and I could go and play for India in different parts of the world. I needed nothing else.'

This is what India is all about. Simplicity and humility meshed with incredible talent. Sakshee did ride an aeroplane and it eventually helped her achieve Olympic glory. Sunelita is now on her way to becoming an Olympian. Soon after winning the Junior Asia Cup, she had said in an interview, 'I dream of going to the Olympics and playing for India. I want to win an Olympics medal for that's what is my ultimate ambition.'

'She has every reason to say that,' argued John. When I asked him why he is so upbeat about Sunelita and what makes her special, John walked me to the Kalinga stadium pitch and picked up a hockey stick. Looking at it intently, he said to me, 'She has speed. She has incredible speed with the ball. She is fit. If you see her pass the ball, you will understand what I am talking about. She almost drag passes the ball. I have hardly ever seen a woman do that. Think of the kind of muscle power and speed it requires and she does it so naturally. She is the Hardik Singh of the women's team and could well be the next big star in Indian hockey.'

Having seen her closely, John knows how good she is and how good she can become. 'At the moment someone has holed in on her as a forward. And she is scoring goals. If you check the Junior Asia Cup she scored some four or five goals for India including the goal against Japan in the final. As a result, she has been identified as a forward. However, she is actually a midfielder. That's the position for her and that's where she belongs. While I am not saying that she will not do well as a forward, I am saying to you that she will do even better as a midfielder,' argued John.

When I asked if he would want to speak to Janneke Schopman, the Indian women's Head Coach, the answer was in the affirmative. 'Yes, because otherwise Sunelita will never do so,' he said with a smile.

Thereafter, David went on to explain how it is important for players from Odisha to express themselves. 'Each of them is an introvert. They hardly ever speak. I always had arguments with Dr Batra on Amit Rohidas. Dr Batra was not sure of his field play and I used to say it was not just about field play. Sandeep Singh wasn't great at field play either. Yet, he was part of the team as a drag flicker. While scoring goals was important, what was equally important was saving goals. And that's what Amit Rohidas can do best. He is one of the best first rushers in the world. I am glad we agreed eventually and see where Amit Rohidas is today. But he would never say it to Dr Batra or to the coach. Unlike the Punjabis who are expressive and would say things if they needed to, players from this area are all very similar and would hardly ever speak. It is the same for Amit, Deep Grace Ekka, Birendra Lakra, Anjali, Jyothi Chatri and now Sunelita. It is a character trait and it needs to change. They need to be more expressive or the Germans, Australians and the Dutch would take advantage,' said John.

Yet again I was transported back to a story that has now achieved folk status in the annals of Indian Olympic sport.

Sindhu had just lost a hard fought first round match at the Australian Open against former world number one and London Olympics silver medallist Yihan Wang in May 2015 and yet coach and mentor Pullela Gopichand wasn't flustered. Sindhu's sister Divya was in Australia and there wouldn't be much scarring from the defeat with family around. Rather, the next few days in Melbourne would be her last few days of enjoyment in 12 months. Gopi, in fact, said as much to Sindhu and all restrictions on food and late nights were removed temporarily. It was party time. The storm before the lull. Merriment before the calm. The last few days before going into hard Olympic labour.

Soon after the duo returned to India, Gopi called

Sindhu to his office in his academy in Gachibowli and handed her a letter. It was a first in their 14-year-long association and listed the 'dos and don'ts' for the next 12 months. And among them was a clause that a 20-year-old youngster would have to surrender her phone to her coach. No phone and no gastronomic indulgence, Gopi was coming down hard on the talented Sindhu. Talent, he argued, needed to be honed to win an Olympic medal and he was determined to leave nothing to chance. 'I had the 2010 Asian Games in mind. While coming back from Guangzhou I had called Sindhu and Ramana (her father) and said I will see you at 4.30 a.m. the next morning. And all she had said was yes. That's what made me feel I could push her more. Yes, I was a little worried about the phone because among all my students she was the fastest to respond to a phone message. Clearly she was hooked on to the gadget. But it was a distraction we could do without,' said Gopi while looking back at those 12 months that eventually made the legend of Sindhu.

The phone wasn't the only thing. More importantly, 'She was very silent on court. Almost as if she did not want to express herself. If you see some of her cohorts like Carolina Marin you will know what I mean. She had to express herself. Give it back. That's how modern sport is, and you can't let you opponents get mentally strong on you,' said Gopi.

'I felt the worst when Gopi Sir made me stand in the middle of the seven courts in the academy in Hyderabad and screamed at me to shout. He wouldn't let me go otherwise. There was no one there and he had never done this before. He was angry and wanted me to be aggressive. I hated it. Hated it all. Hated him and what I was being asked to do. And I started crying but wasn't able to shout,' smiled Sindhu as she looked back at what all she did with fondness.

But then she did shout. She was pushed to it by her coach. And with her, all of India too had found a voice. Since then, she has always been expressive, and it added a very different dimension to her game.

It could do the same for Sunelita if she starts to express herself. Perhaps walk up to her coach and suggest she is more comfortable playing midfield rather than playing upfront. 'There is no harm in trying. If Janneke then decides no she is better off as forward, she can always play forward. But all I am saying is she should be expressive and not hold back,' said John.

As we were starting to walk back to his office, he looked at me and said with a smile. 'Such talents don't come too often,' he added. 'She is one. She can make a real difference to Indian women's hockey if she is nurtured and looked after well. Speed, power, skill, she has them all. And that's rare for anyone I can tell you that. And when you think she wasn't even a hockey player just about 18 months back and has just turned 16, you think it is unreal. That's what talent identification should be about and that's what we need to do more here in Odisha. A few more Sunelitas for India, and you could well be in line to winning the Olympic medal that India so narrowly missed in Tokyo despite being the fittest team in the competition.'

The Rugby girls

It was 5:52 a.m. in the morning and the sun was already out in Kolkata. It wasn't really hot yet and there was an early morning breeze adding to the serenity of the morning. That's when Akshay, who heads marketing for Rugby India, called me saying he was waiting for us at the main gate of the SAI Center within the Vivekananda Yuva Bharati Krirangan complex in Kolkata. I was actually two minutes away from the stadium and was just taking the final turn from the Beliaghata crossing to enter the complex. I must say I was excited. It was a special invite from Rahul Bose, President of Rugby India, and it is always a matter of great excitement to see young women, who are aspiring to make a mark in international sport for the country, get ready for a major competition. Rahul messaged saying there was an issue with his car and he would be there no later than 6:45 a.m. As my car took the turn towards football maidan 2, the training base for Rugby India ahead of the Asian Games, I had my first look at the Indian women's team.

Unlike what I had seen a year earlier, the girls were no longer just five feet tall. A number of them seemed taller and heavier, and most of them were now 5'6' or more. It is finally a Rugby team rather than Gymnastics or Kho Kho. As I entered the ground with permission from Ludwiche van Deventer, the coach from South Africa who has now been associated with Indian Rugby for five years, he was busy shouting out instructions to the physio and the support team to place the training equipment for the girls to do a specific run-and-jump drill. Hurdles, which are a feet high, were placed and Ludwiche asked all the girls to line up and start the drill. That's when Rahul arrived and after we exchanged pleasantries, he said to me that it might help if he identified the girls to me and added a little on each of their backgrounds. The plan was for me to speak to them after training and the background information would be of great help.

Among the ones picked in the team to go to Hangzhou, there were four girls from Odisha, the maximum from any state. 'The kind of work being done in Odisha is spectacular,' said Rahul. 'They have realised that if it is Bollywood which is the equivalent of soft power in

Mumbai, in Odisha it is sport. With the government supporting the sport with passion and commitment, we can now see results.'

Just as he was speaking, Hupi Majhi, one of the seniors in the team, performed the drill to perfection. As Coach Ludwiche shouted out some praise and performance analyst Rasta mentioned how she has continued to improve in the last few months, Rahul started to tell me her story. 'Would you believe it that no one in her village knew she played Rugby till 2017?' he said with a wry smile. 'This is because her parents were seriously against her playing and in a conservative village where no woman is allowed to wear shorts, playing Rugby was a far cry. She decided not to tell anyone and just pursued her passion.'

Hupi is a lean and strong girl and has a poise about herself. Among the group of four from Odisha, she is the leader. When we all got together for breakfast at the end of training at the SAI hostel opposite the training facility, it was almost natural that she stood at the centre taking control of the interaction.

'Have you eaten something?' she asked me in Hindi before starting to fiddle with her phone. 'I have seen you somewhere. Are you connected to Sachin Sir?'

I was seriously intrigued. When I asked her how and where had she seen me with Sachin Tendulkar, she said, 'On Facebook. There are pictures of the two of you and when Rahul Sir mentioned that you are coming to take our interview, I was looking at Facebook to find out a little more about you.'

Here is a girl whose village, literally, has a few hundred families who are all farmers and where no one had ever heard of Facebook till a few years earlier.

'I was a very shy girl and did not really know how to speak or interact with people,' she said. 'When I was sent to boarding school in Bhubaneshwar in 2007, I was scared. I did not want to expose my weaknesses. That's why in my initial days I did not attend too many classes. In the school mess, it often happened that I did not ask for food because I couldn't speak. So I went hungry.'

By that time, I was all ears and just waited for her to continue.

'It was only after I joined KISS, Kalinga Institute of Social Sciences, the world's first and only tribal university, that I heard of Rugby. In fact, it was at KISS that I first saw people play the sport and I was attracted to it. It seemed something I could do well in and something where I could be my own self. I don't need to speak much when playing. Shouting out instructions yes, but all that came much later. I started playing rugby because it allowed me to do something without having to speak much.'

'So did you tell your parents about your new passion?' I asked.

'I did but they were not willing to let me play,' said Hupi. 'In our village, women aren't allowed to play any form of outdoor sport. Growing up in Dhatika, north of Kendujhar, I was only allowed to go to school as a kind of outdoor activity. The rest of the time I was at home and the norm was to get girls married after they turned 17-18. Sport was out of the question. So, when I mentioned I wanted to play rugby, my parents were angry. They felt I was letting the entire village down and did not want to confront the rest of the community. So I decided to tell them that I wasn't playing anymore and just silently continued to pursue my dream.'

With each sentence, her voice was turning louder. It was clear that she was keen on telling her story as much as I was keen on listening to her.

'There was no risk,' she continued. 'I never imagined that I could play for India and unless you do so, there was never any fear of my parents knowing that I was a rugby player. They wouldn't ever come to see me at KISS and I could get away doing what I wanted to do till they got me married. But then it all changed when I was given an opportunity to play for India. Honestly, it was a dream come true. Wearing the national jersey and doing what I always wanted to do, get on an airplane and travel the world, it seemed rugby was giving me things I had never imagined I could lay my hands on. The truth is rugby has taught me everything.'

She paused to sip some water, and then continued. 'The problem arose when we finished runner-up in the Asia Rugby Women's Seven's tournament in Laos,' said Hupi. 'I had played very well and in one game managed a joint highest six tries. You can say I had helped my team to the runner-up position. When we came back to Odisha, the local papers published my pictures. That's when the penny dropped. I went home for a break and my parents were shocked to learn that I was a rugby player. They had seen the pictures and it wasn't pleasant.'

It was a very Mary Kom-like story. In Mary's case, she had to change her name to Mary from Chungneizang Mangte to avoid getting reprimanded at home for trying out boxing and it was when her picture was published in the local press that the truth was out. Her father did administer a thrashing but could never stop her from pursuing her dreams.

Hupi too was doing the same. 'What changed everything was the support from the Government of Odisha,' she said, with real emotion in her voice. 'The government had announced a reward of a few lac rupees for each one of us. In our family no one had ever heard of that kind of money. We were poor people and lacs of rupees were a pipe dream. When the money was transferred to our accounts and I handed over the money to my parents, they were stunned. Initially it was a sense of disbelief. How could I earn so much money playing rugby! It was not something they had ever imagined and all of a sudden, things changed. They too realised that rugby was doing their daughter good. It was a means to some kind of mobility and my family was happy. Now my parents are all delighted to know I play rugby for India and the whole village are converts. When I go there, they organise felicitations for me and young children are sent to me to seek my blessings. Rugby has given me all I have in life.'

'What about marriage?' I asked. More so because she is 28 now, considered way too old for girls in her village to get married.

'No one now asks me the marriage question,' she said. 'And even if they do, I will say no. I want to play for India for a few more years and there is no question of getting married at the moment. The sport is my dream and with Rahul Sir and Rugby India doing what they are with the support of the Government of Odisha, we can see the sport going in the right direction. We now have a team of 10 Support Staff, a Head Coach, an Assistant Coach, a Physio, a Nutritionist, a Masseur and honestly it is all being done extremely well. None of the girls have anything to complain about. Our camps are well organised and not just that we are also paid at the end of every camp. You tell me—should I leave all this and get married? Rather, if I play for a few more years, I will be in a position to do things my way even after I am married. And in any case, I am the one who is the lead bread winner in the family at the moment. Rugby has made it possible so there is no question of leaving my sport.'

As Hupi was telling me her story, I was just thinking back to the power of sport. A contact sport, rugby, has forced a village where girls did not even wear shorts and venture out in the open, to change their outlook and celebrate their own. A number of girls in Dhatika are now playing rugby in an attempt to become the next Hupi Majhi. Her mother who was once worried what would happen to her daughter if she got injured while playing rugby is now perfectly okay with her having some bruises or a broken nose while playing. 'My mother now knows injuries can happen in rugby and its fine,' Hupi said with a smile on her face. 'While she doesn't want me to get injured or have my nose broken, if something happens, she wouldn't panic.'

While there is an element of Nikhat Zareen to this part of the story, the message is clear. Rugby has given her the opportunity to make a difference and because of the support coming her way from Rugby India and the Government of Odisha, she can now be the beacon of change for an entire generation of girls in Keonjhar. She is already a star. Having won medals at the national and international level, Hupi is an aspirational tale for every girl who wants to pursue a career in sport. More importantly for every parent whose daughter wants to play sport.

As Shri Naveen Patnaik says, 'Sport for Youth and Youth for Future'.

Dumuni Marndi, Mama Naik and Tarulata Naik

As Hupi was telling me her story, Mama Naik, Tarulata Naik and Dumuni Marndi, all part of the Asian Games Rugby Seven's national team, were listening intently. Each of them had very similar stories to tell. Dumuni, all but 5 feet, doesn't even look a rugby player.

'Don't you feel scared when you play against girls literally double your size?' I asked.

'When I joined the team, I had asked this question of our coach,' she replied. 'He told me that if the Japanese can play as well as they do, why can't I compete with girls who are bigger and stronger? It is not just about your build. It is also about what you believe in.'

Here is a young woman from a village, which had no tradition of sport, now determined to play for India at the Olympics. No one from her family has ever heard of or played rugby. And yet we now have a Dumuni Marndi.

'I did not know of rugby while growing up,' she said.

'It was only after I came to KISS that I heard of the sport. When I enrolled in KISS, a team of seniors had just come back from an international assignment. That was my first initiation into the sport. If they could do so, why can't I? I asked this question of myself almost regularly before trying out rugby. I soon started playing and may I say for the first time felt I was doing something worthwhile in life.'

There was a pause and it seemed she was getting a bit emotional.

'See, for us, there is nothing to look forward to in life,' she said. 'Girls in our village all have the same life. You don't do much while growing up and it is all about helping the men in the family. And when you are off a certain age, your parents will get you married. Then you have children and do the same that your elders did. Life is the same for everyone and you just go through the motions.

'In all this, the one thing missing is RESPECT. Girls don't have respect. Yes, we aren't ill-treated or anything. But do people look at us with respect? No. That's what I wanted to earn for myself and that's what rugby has given us. When I play, it is me and what I want to do or can achieve. It is not what my parents or village elders have told me. It is not what my brothers want. It is what I want. I want to be on the pitch for India. I am happy to get injured. It is my will and my life. And with Rugby India giving us money, no one in the family can say a word anymore.'

Clearly, a rebel was speaking out.

Mama Naik and Tarulata Naik concurred. 'People don't really know what sport can do,' said Mama. 'Without any kind of exposure, they have no idea what rugby is all about. For them, it is about people banging into each other and ending up with bruised arms and legs. They have no idea about the science behind the sport. That it can be a career is not something anyone in our villages have ever known or heard. That's why when we got selected into the Indian team, there was an element of surprise to it. No one had ever imagined something like this was possible.

'The real change happened when we started getting paid. Everyone wants a better life and there is no harm in that. You want to eat one extra egg if you want to. Have an extra glass of milk or have one extra piece of fish. For years, we did not have the means to do this. Each time I wanted to have an extra roti I would have to think that my mother could go hungry if I did so. It is not a very good feeling. While she won't say much, as a responsible daughter you need to take care of your mother as your primary responsibility. Now things have changed. If she wants to have milk or fish or eggs or dal, we can afford it.

Sometimes girls from the village come to our house and we all have a meal together. They see me and think if I can provide my family with a better life, they too can do the same. Each one of them now want to play sport and most importantly no one stops them anymore.'

Clearly, Odisha has done something right. By setting up KISS and providing tribal girls the opportunity to educate themselves, the government has been able to bring about a sea change. And with sport taking centre stage at KISS, the Rugby Girls can now lead a revolution once considered unthinkable. With Rugby India getting reasonable support from the Government of Odisha and with a proactive President like Bose at the helm, things can only get better for Indian Rugby in the future. Hupi Majhi, Mama Naik, Dumuni Marndi and Tarulata Naik will no longer be aberrations going forward. Rather, they are now the benchmark with many looking at them as role models and success stories, who have proved that dreams do come true.

WORLD CLASS INFRASTRUCTURE

Our athletes can now train in India

On May 31, 2023 Chief Minister Shri Naveen Patnaik reviewed the progress on the manifesto commitments and achievements of the Sports & Youth Services Department over the last four years.

It was Tusharkanti Behera, the Sports & Youth Services Minister, who presented a detailed development report on the transformative initiatives undertaken by the department for achieving the targets. In fact, when I met the Sports Minister at the Kalinga Stadium on July 14, 2023, he was emphatic in asserting Odisha's commitment to sport. As the sun was shining bright on a dazzling Kalinga Stadium, Shri Behera sounded supremely confident when saying, 'The Hon. CM has made sports a priority. We are committed to traveling this journey together and making Odisha the nerve centre of Indian sport in the years to come.'

As mentioned at the start, Shri Behera had already apprised the Chief Minister that Odisha has now emerged as a favoured destination for sports owing to its exceptional infrastructure, world standard human capital and successful organization of numerous global sporting competitions. 'Under the CM's leadership, the state is actively promoting and nurturing a wide range of sports, propelling its journey as a flourishing sports hub,' the report read.

Odisha, it is now recognised, is the global hub for hockey, having successfully organized consecutive editions of the FIH Hockey World Cup in 2018 and 2023. Furthermore, Odisha has been the venue for prominent hockey events like the FIH Hockey Junior Men's World Cup, Pro League, FIH Olympic Qualifiers, and FIH Series Finals, solidifying its position as a global destination for the sport. The Kalinga Hockey Stadium and the Birsa Munda Hockey Stadium are the best hockey stadiums in the world.

Odisha has also made remarkable strides in hosting noteworthy international events in other sports. In football, the state successfully organized the FIFA U17 Women's World Cup and the SAFF U20 Championship, providing talented young footballers from around the world with a platform to showcase their skills. On November 21, 2023 the state hosted the world cup qualifier between India and Qatar in front of a sold out crowd. Kalinga Stadium in Bhubaneswar also serves as the home ground for Odisha FC, the reigning Super Cup Champions.

Odisha Open, Commonwealth Table Tennis Championships and a plethora of national events across sports have redefined the story of Odisha as a sports hub in India. In kho kho, the Odisha Juggernauts is the state's franchise in the Ultimate Kho Kho League.

Odisha has been able to do all this and more by launching a series of High Performance Centers across various sports disciplines in collaboration with corporates and eminent sportspersons, in a unique public-private partnership model that is now being replicated widely across India. It has not only extended its support to Hockey India for another 10 years, it is also supporting National Federations in football, rugby, kho kho and swimming.

In addition to the Birsa Munda Hockey Stadium, Rourkela, which has earned a place in the Guinness Book of World Records, Odisha houses other sporting venues such as the Birsa Munda Athletics Stadium in Rourkela, the Kalinga Stadium Tennis Center, Dharanidhar Sports Complex in Keonjhar amongst others, providing athletes with top-tier facilities to train and excel in their respective disciplines.

Recognizing the significance of grassroots development, the Odisha Government has taken proactive measures to nurture young talent and establish a strong foundation for sports in the region. As part of this initiative, 22 astro-turf hockey fields have been set up across the Sundargarh district alone. This strategic move aims to identify and nurture promising talent, ensuring the sustained growth and success of the sport. Moreover, the state is establishing 90 multipurpose indoor stadiums in urban areas. Six FIFA standard pitches have also been installed.

Over the last four years, the sports budget has been raised to Rs 1217 Crores reflecting the commitment of Odisha and its Chief Minister towards sports development and promotion.

Throwing light on sports development in the state, the sports minister had argued, 'Odisha has come a long way in sports and is fully committed to fostering a vibrant sports culture. We aim to encourage talent, inspire future generations, and position Odisha as a leading sports destination in India.'

How it all started: The process

None of this could have happened overnight. When the CM first announced the setting up of a High Performance Centre for Athletics in 2017 during the Asian Athletics Championship, the seeds of a sporting revolution was sown. The Chief Minister believed in a model of partnerships which is critical for the sports field to grow and flourish. Soon officers from Odisha reached out to the corporates willing to partner with the government for sports development. The government was in a position to allocate large funds for building the infrastructure, while the corporates were requested to put together best of the coaches and support staff to run professional high-performance coaching programs in the newly created sports facilities.

The government wasn't equipped to select the best coaches or offer the best scientific training. It was not something the government can do or invest in. Rather, the government was there to offer funding and infrastructure and it was agreed that the state would be reaching out to leading corporates of the country who had an interest in developing sport to work in partnership. Basis this decision, the government reached out to the Tatas to partner in the setting up of a Hockey HPC, Reliance to set up an athletics HPC, JSW for a swimming HPC,

Aditya Birla Group and Gagan Narang for a shooting HPC, Abhinav Bindra Foundation for a Sports Science HPC and so on. These corporates and individual athletes are responsible for providing the best coaches and technical expertise to these HPC's while the government is responsible for providing infrastructure and funding. It is this public-private partnership model that has driven Odisha sport in the last six years between 2017 and 2023.

The story of the Hockey HPC

The foundation stone of the Hockey HPC was laid on August 13, 2019 by Shri Naveen Patnaik and Shri TV Narendran, the MD of Tata Steel. The Tata group has proven expertise in promoting hockey and has for decades invested in nurturing local talent. The idea behind the HPC was simple. At one level, it aimed to harness local talent from the region, and in doing so, showcase the state nationally. While at another, it aimed to create and nurture a strong sports culture. It started with 30 girls under the age of 17 and has now increased its strength to 45 and has also added an equal number of boys to the roster. The idea is to go up to a maximum number of 50 girls and boys each. Each student is offered residential facilities and access to modern scientific training imparted by the best coaches and by the time they are done with their stints at the HPC, the best of them are absorbed by the national camps.

'We started in August 2019 with 30 students and the plan was to add to the number by the next year. But then Covid hit and everything was impacted in a manner than none of us could have ever envisaged. It was only after the world had started to get back that we added boys to our roster in January 2021,' said Rajeev Seth, the man in charge of the Naval Tata HPC in Bhubaneshwar.

During Covid this was a rare institution that managed to keep going without having to shut down. 'We asked our students if they wanted to stay on or go back home. We also needed to plan if it was safer for them to stay on in what was a much more controlled environment or was it better for them to go home to the villages where the best medical facilities aren't available and there was very little testing going on,' argued Seth.

The students were told that they had to do everything on their own, from mopping to washing clothes to cleaning the HPC because outside contact had to be minimised. This was the only way the HPC could be kept functional. The Kalinga Stadium, which sees a lot of human inflow and outflow on a daily basis with a lot of construction work going on, was totally closed down and there was no outside contact with the students of the HPC. This meant that the only human contact for the students was with each other and with regular testing, training could go on uninterrupted.

'This was a very difficult period. We needed to get this right. And thankfully we did. The students were determined to stay on and make every kind of sacrifice. It is because of their willingness and determination that things worked to plan,' said Rajeev Seth.

Soon after things started to open up and Hockey India decided to host an academy tournament on the lines of the nationals, the Naval Tata HPC team won the competition against the likes of Haryana and UP, teams with bigger reputations in Indian hockey. 'This could only happen because our girls were never out of training. As a result, they were in shape throughout and it was on display in this tournament. It had a serious impact in giving the players confidence and all of a sudden the focus was on Odisha and what the state was doing in sport,' argued Seth.

The reason why the Naval Tata Hockey HPC works to perfection is because the government has been able to back it up with the establishment of multiple grassroot centres, which act as the supply chain for talent. Had there been no grassroot centres, there was no way the HPC could keep getting the kind of talented students it does. The laying out of a huge number of turf pitches across the state, more than 3/4ths of which is in

Sundargarh alone, has helped the sport hugely. It means that the students from these grassroot centres now have access to artificial turf pitches from the very start of their careers and by the time they move to the HPC they are used to playing on astro turf and also exposed to the modern methods of training and sports science. What it also means is that the HPC administrators do not need to go out scouting talent. It is already being done through the grassroot centres and there is a perfect synergy established between grassroot sport and elite high-performance sport.

'When we played there was hardly any facility at hand. We did not have astro turfs across the state and grew up playing on pebble fields. This made it harder for us to make the transition to synthetic turf at a later stage in our careers. As kids if you are exposed to a particular kind of facility, you will always find it difficult to adapt to something entirely new at an advanced age. That's where the youngsters of today have an advantage. In Sundargarh district alone there are a huge number of turf pitches. Cuttack too will soon have a turf pitch and there will be one more in Bhubaneswar. From Day 1, the youngsters are training on these pitches. They know what it is to play on these pitches and have no problems in adapting when they move to the HPC and then to the national camps,' argued Dilip Tirkey, President of

Hockey India and perhaps the greatest player to come out of Sundargarh.

'These students also use GPS technology, which is used by the Indian national team. There are many sports federations in the country, which still don't have access to this technology. It gives you an idea how far advanced these kids are when compared to some of our senior athletes. Except the cricketers who have access to GPS technology, the footballers from the leading ISL clubs and Hockey India, others still don't use this technology for regular training,' argued one of the coaches employed by the Naval Tata HPC.

Technology, it must be acknowledged, is expensive. And it is not always possible for national federations which are cash strapped to use technology for grassroot sport. Had it not been for the support of the Odisha Government, it would have been impossible for young men and women at the sub-junior and junior level to use GPS technology for training.

'It is not about subjectivity. And nor is it just about skill. Modern hockey is very different and you need to be physically able to cope up with the pace of the game. And the only way we know someone is good enough is when we have all the objective data in front of us. Earlier a player could come and accuse the coach of bias and say he or she had put in his best and there was no way that he or she was not up to it physically. It would be awkward because it was the coach's word against the players. There was always that grey area, which could complicate things. Now everything is data driven and we can measure every little detail and only if someone is physically adept can he or she progress further in the sport,' explained David John, the Head of the Hockey HPC in the state. John, who has coached the Indian team before, was the man behind the improved fitness of the national team in Tokyo, which won the bronze after a gap of 41 years.

Sitting in his ground floor office at the Kalinga Stadium, John was watching the kids train from his window. Each of them had a small black GPS device fitted into them and that's what John was pointing out to us. 'Can you see that?' he asked. 'That's how we use modern technology. These girls are no more than 13-14 and they already know how to use this (GPS). So when they graduate to the national camp and are exposed to foreign coaches, they will have no problems in adjusting to the training methods used there,' he said proudly.

'A lot of people think we want these students to be scholars and that's why we push them to study. That was never the intention and nor is it the true picture. I am happy even if they get 45 per cent and pass. We encourage them to pursue their studies because they need to be able to comprehend technology. To do so, you need basic education. You need to understand where these students come from. They are mostly tribal kids who only know how to play hockey and want to continuously play hockey. They haven't a clue what is too much or too little. If you let them be, they will come and play all night if you know what I mean. That's when we need to counsel them and speak to them and make them understand what is good for them. We show them the data and now they know what physical parameters they need to maintain to be able to perform at their optimum,' said Seth.

'Each of them are paid a stipend and that has helped a lot. For some of them eating one good meal a day was an ordeal. Their families have found it hard in the past to make ends meet. So when they go home for a break, a number of them find it hard to maintain the standard of nutrition available in the HPC. It means when they come back, we have to yet again work on them to get them back to shape. Sometimes students have come back 6-7 kgs lighter and it has taken weeks and months to get the same person back into shape.

Now we have been able to change things. Each is given a diet chart with details of what is expected of them and they follow the chart even when they are at home for a break. With the stipend, they can buy the required vegetables and fruits and pulses and things have now become much easier. Also, with the money they are able to take care of the families basic dietary needs and it gives them a sense of pride and empowerment,' argues John.

Just as he finished speaking did a young girl score a really good goal in the practice game that was being played. She just ran in from the wings and anticipated the pass to perfection before unleashing a powerful flick into the goal.

'Earlier she wouldn't get the ball. The tendency was to showcase your skill and dribble through the maximum number of players. Everyone would try to do the same and there was no teamwork. Have you seen the film *Chak De! India*? You remember what was going on between Komal Chautala and Preeti Sabbarwal in the film? That's actually what happens unless you tell them it's wrong. In a team sport there is never one individual hero. It is always a collective. You need to instil it in them from a very young age that modern hockey is different. It is not about how good you are with the hockey stick. It is as important just how good you are without the hockey stick and in terms of fitness. Everything can be quantified and is objective. That's how far advanced the sport is and that's what we are trying to achieve in the HPC,' said John.

When I asked him if we could go to the pitch and

observe the girls train, he was happy to give us permission and even accompanied us outside. As we were standing and enjoying the action unfold, one of the girls ran up to one of the trainers and asked, 'Didi mera score kya tha?'

The moment she did so, I could see a smile on John's face. 'Ten years back you did not hear about the Yo-Yo test. Passing the Yo-Yo doesn't make you a better hockey player. But what it does is it equips you to be a more complete player. Only if you are fit enough and that's what the Yo-Yo and other tests help measure, can you showcase your skill as a player. One is not exclusive of the other. Rather, there is perfect synergy between the two. A fit player is a better player. He or she can be in the game for longer and towards the very end of the match not get tired and make mistakes. If you are physically tired, you can never be mentally switched on and that's when mistakes happen. If you see records, there are many instances of India conceding a late goal and missing out on very important wins. Now with technology available you can measure every parameter and that can help the player immensely. A fitter player can subsequently improve on the skill set going forward. But if you don't have the necessary fitness, the sport is not for you. However skilled you may be, you need to be fit enough to make a mark in modern hockey,' John was emphatic.

'When you add this quality of infrastructure (pointing to the pitch at the Kalinga Stadium) to the modern scientific training methods we are employing, you know you are doing something right. Huge credit to the government for letting us do this,' he concluded.

To note that out of the total of 115 astro turf pitches in the country, more than 30 will be in Odisha stand testimony to the investment in infrastructure. And some of these pitches were imported during Covid when supply chain disruption was a feature of life. The government did not leave any stone unturned to get the pitches imported and the effort is now seeing a serious spurt in participation levels across the state. More such efforts are in the pipeline and could only help strengthen the foundation of the sport going forward.

Most importantly, the effort is not just restricted to hockey. In athletics, yet another sport where Odisha has a strong tradition, it is another India shining story with the Reliance HPC housed at the Kalinga Stadium precinct leading the way.

Athletics—'We can break the 10 second barrier in 100 meters': Rehan Basha

The Odisha Reliance Foundation Athletics HPC, is a collaborative effort of the Odisha Government and

Reliance Foundation. It was set up with the aim of improving the standard of athletics across the state and produce home-grown athletes who can achieve both national and international success.

The HPC is part of Shri Naveen Patnaik's vision, investment and efforts in making sports and its infrastructure a priority sector and a dedicated effort towards creating a holistic ecosystem that benefits sport and its athletes. With the athlete at the core of this vision, the facility now has every kind of modern infrastructure a track and field star needs to succeed at the global level. Operating out of Kalinga stadium in Bhubaneswar, training 50+ athletes across disciplines, the HPC aims to become Asia's most innovative High-Performance Athletics Centre in the years to come. While winning medals at key international competitions is a long-term goal, the HPC is currently focusing on the holistic development of the athletes through an integrated approach, a combination of physical, mental, and psychological training, setting an example that other academies across the country can follow to fuel India's sporting ambition.

To ensure Indian athletes receive world-class support in the crucial aspect of Sports Science & Medicine, the team includes experts from Sir HN Reliance Foundation Hospital in Mumbai that work with the athletes in areas such as strength and conditioning coaching, physiotherapy support for injury prevention and rehab, sports nutrition, sports psychology, and biomechanics assessment. The key facilities provided to the athletes in the Odisha Reliance Foundation High Performance Center includes hostel, gym, treatment room, athletics gear/ kit, recreation, etc.

It is headed by James Hillier, one of the best domain experts in the world and one who has been full time associated with the HPC from November 2019. 'I was working on the project from 12 months prior and travelled to India multiple times between 2018 and 2019. Thereafter, I moved base to India at the end of 2019 with a dream to making India a strong track and field nation. I have said this on record and I repeat that there is enormous talent in India. But then there is talent in many other countries of the world as well. A lot of this talent never get an opportunity. That's what we are doing in this Reliance-Government of Odisha HPC for Athletics. We are providing opportunities to the talented young athletes of the state and beyond to make them national and international champions,' said Hillier.

'When I first came to Odisha there was no tradition of scientific training. In fact, the two excellent tracks were hardly used. I wouldn't be wrong in saying no one used them. The first time I went there to check out the facilities there was not a single athlete on the track. Now you will find them full with a lot of young men and women starting to believe they can make a career in athletics. With six international medals already, the HPC has come a long way from where we started. It has been a lot of hard work. Laying a strong foundation was the early aim. That's what is always the key. When you build a house, laying the foundation is what takes time. Now is the time for the final paint and to put up the pictures on the walls when it all starts to look good,' he argued.

On the day that Hillier and I were speaking about the HPC, Jyothi Yarraji, a product of the center, was competing in the finals of the University Games in China. She had made the finals with a very good time of 12.98 and despite the rain put in a very strong effort to win the gold in her maiden appearance. Hillier, understandably, was delighted. 'She has come a long way. While she is nowhere a finished product just yet, the progress is noticeable. At the Asian level she is now a medal contender at any meet. The next step will be to take that final jump and start making impact at the global level,' he argued.

Articulating the process, he explained in detail how the HPC functions. 'My job is to ensure the athlete delivers on the final 3-4 per cent which makes the ultimate difference at the international level. I am focussed on the elite high-performance athlete. There are coaches who do something fundamentally different. They work on young men and women in schools and their job is to enthuse them into taking up athletics. They provide us with the supply line. Once you have a steady supply of talented men and women, it is only a matter of time before you have someone who will alter the entire landscape of athletics in the country,' he argued.

Yet again what worked to the advantage of this HPC was Covid. 'Yes you can say that. In a very strange way, Covid helped us bond better and get better. This is because we had planned for it. We were seeing the developments globally and was prepared for the lockdown. We had created a detailed blueprint on what we needed to do and created a bubble within the Kalinga Stadium. I had added assistant coaches and a physio into the bubble and the athletes did not meet a single person from outside. Even I wasn't allowed in. I was living outside with my wife and family in Bhubaneshwar and would coach them using technology. That the HPC could be kept functional with the coaches and trainers all inside with the athletes made a huge difference,' he argued.

The Reliance Foundation under Mrs Ambani has left no stone unturned in giving the youth of Odisha and the rest of India the best facilities available at a global scale. With the best of human capital now associated with the

HPC, results have started to flow and will only get better in the months to come.

Just as I was finishing my conversation with James Hillier did news come in that Jyothi had won gold braving some serious inclement weather. There were a lot of high-fives around and each one of the athletes standing by felt a sense of pride. One of them, young Rehan Basha, who is considered to be hugely talented made the most telling comment. 'We will soon start winning medals at the Olympics. 2028 is the target. Jyothi will only get better. And in the sprint we will also break the 10-second barrier. You will see Amlan break this barrier soon,' he said.

As he was speaking, there was real passion in his voice and a glint in his eye. He clearly believed in what he was saying. An Indian sprint athlete running a sub-10-second race would be historic and if Rehan's confidence is anything to go by, it can indeed happen in the next few years.

Frankly, this is what Hillier was alluding to. Earlier, we had the talent. India always had an Amlan or a Jyothi or a Rehan Basha waiting in the wings. What we did not have was an institution where such talent could be honed. Thanks to the Reliance Foundation and the Government of Odisha, we now have an athletics HPC which can compete in quality with any center in any part of the world. That's where Odisha has been able to make change and lead the way. With other states stepping up to emulate the Odisha model, we could soon see Indian athletics turn the corner.

In the words of Amlan Borgohain, 'I joined Odisha Reliance Foundation Athletics High Performance Centre in February 2020. Luckily due to the pandemic, I had six months of training and the team here helped to build my foundation first. I always believe the athletes' foundation needs to be very strong. I started taking part in several events in 2021. I won the Federation Cup with a timing of 10.44 seconds in 2021 and then in the Warangal Nationals, the timing dipped to 10.34 seconds. The technical aspects too changed like maintaining postures and running on the curve along with the eating habits.'

Hailing from Assam, Amlan initially started off as a footballer and he even made it to the National level. However, encouragement from friends and family steered him to a more fulfilling direction after his football career was cut short by a number of injuries. One day a friend of his elder brother showed him an advertisement for an athletics app in a newspaper and asked him to shift to athletics.

With one simple decision and a lot of hard work, Amlan found himself with the 100m and 200m men's titles at the National games, and prior to that broke the 100m national record at the All India Inter-Railway Athletics Championships and at the Federation Cup. The 25-year-old set a new national record in the men's 200m with a time of 20.52 seconds.

Now with Hillier as coach, Amlan, as Rehan Basha says is training to become India's best ever sprinter of all time. With strong performances under his belt, he ran for India in the Asian Games in Hangzhou.

If the Hockey and Athletics HPC are both aimed at providing the country with elite high-performance stars, as are the others which we have written about in the previous chapter, it is but natural that there will be injures and other concerns calling for urgent intervention in helping with recovery. That's where sports science takes centre stage. It is no surprise therefore that the Government of Odisha has partnered with the Abhinav Bindra Foundation in setting up the sports science HPC in the same Kalinga Stadium precinct where athletes from across sports disciplines can now come for support and recovery. Interestingly, as mentioned earlier, my team and I also tried out some of the machines and enjoyed every bit of the experience.

DECODING THE ODISHA MODEL

The key to the success of the Odisha model has been the synergy between all stakeholders involved. Sports administrators heading the respective national federations, members of the bureaucracy, athletes and corporates have all come together in creating and then consistently improving the template. And it all happens through dialogue. Transparency and accountability are the watchwords, and every critical feedback is taken into account to further improve and get better. So, when the three of us, Dilip Tirkey, R. Vineel Krishna and Boria Majumdar, sat down over multiple steaming hot cups of tea against the backdrop of a rain soaked Kalinga Stadium in one of the conference rooms of this fantastic facility, the conversation addressed key learnings from past experience and also tried to discuss the template for the way forward.

Boria: Dilip *Bhai,* as someone who is from this region and has scaled great heights in international sport, how do you see your state taking giant strides in becoming the sports capital of India?

Dilip Tirkey: Firstly, let me tell you all this looks like a fairy tale to me at times. To see this kind of work being done in Odisha for sport is the best thing I could have ever hoped for. Let me take you back to how I started. At that time in the late 1980s and early 1990s, all I would look for are grass fields. There was no turf pitch or any such thing. As a young boy who wanted to play hockey, all I would seek out was a grass field, which was somewhat even so that I could practice skill development. I would do some fitness drills on my own and do skill training. That's all I did at the time. When I was part of the Indian set up and in the national camp, I would continue to do my own fitness and skill training and let me tell you emphatically, there was nothing of the kind of facilities that we see here today. No one even expected anything of the like. The change has been incredible and I am very proud to see this transformation being led by my own state.

R. Vineel Krishna: What is important is how quickly this transformation has come about. It is not even a decade that the Honourable Chief Minister decided to take up sport as a means to showcasing Odisha to the world. It all started, as we have documented elsewhere in the book, with the Asian Athletics Championship in 2017. It was the success of this one initiative that demonstrated what sport can do. And that's what started our journey with sport here in Odisha. A decade and a half earlier the sports department used to have a budget of 50 crores or 100 crores at best. Now the budget has gone up to 1300 crores and can go up to 1500 crores in the immediate future. The budget, may I say, is the most fundamental yardstick to prove how serious the state is about sport. For the CM it is not just talk. He always walks the talk and that's what we all do in Odisha. We now have multiple High Performance Centers, grassroot centres, multi-purpose indoor stadiums and other infrastructure that can help drive Indian sports ahead in the future. And things will only get better going forward.

Boria: This is incredible when we note it is a six-year-old story so far! The Odisha I used to come to as a child growing up in neighbouring Bengal and the Odisha I see now are chalk and cheese. If you are an Indian sports analyst, it is a case study of what can happen with serious effort and determination.

Dilip bhai in your case you had to play on grass while growing up and then had to make the transition to artificial turf. How difficult is it to do so and how much of an impact do you think it will make now that we have 20 plus turf pitches in Sundargarh district alone?

Dilip: It can be the defining change in Indian hockey. I see three things happening here in Odisha under the guidance of our Honourable CM Naveen Patnaik ji. First is the creation of necessary infrastructure. Without quality infrastructure there is no sport. You need facilities for people to come and train on, for broadcasters to showcase and for sport to improve. The quality of infrastructure Odisha now has, is the best in the world and that's what has readied the state for its growth story. The second is the hosting of events. If you see the number of events staged in Odisha over the last few years, you will know what I am talking about. In hockey, we have staged multiple sub-junior and junior events in Odisha, we have staged matches of the pro league and most importantly we have hosted two back to back World Cups. Such events get people involved with the sport and help make a serious difference. Finally, we are seeing serious investment in coaching and sports science. You mentioned Sundargarh. In Sundargarh, hockey is a craze among the locals. They love the sport and the participation rate is high. What the state has done is it has established grassroot coaching centres in 16 of the

17 blocks in the district. And each centre is equipped with proper coaching staff who have access to sports science. Add the number of turf pitches in Sundargarh and you will know how important the entire process is. The aspiring youngster can now play on turf pitches from the very beginning and has access to the best coaching and technical expertise. As a result, he will grow up knowing what it is like to play on these pitches and what it is like using modern equipment. When he or she makes the transition to the state or national training programmes, it is a seamless transition. That's what will help the sport get better in India going forward.

Vineel: When we tried to assess how hockey is played in Europe or Australia, the countries that have dominated the sport in the last two decades, we realised that the sport is mainly played in clubs, which have artificial pitches. That's where young men and women come and play and get better. From the very start of their careers, they have access to these artificial turfs. In India, that wasn't the case. Our youngsters would play on mud or pebbled fields and that's how they acquired the initial skill for the sport. It was only when they were called up to the state or the national programme that they would have access to artificial pitches. The transition wasn't easy. The base had already been prepared on grass. And now all of a sudden they were being told to play on these pitches and compete with European teams who had a head start. It wasn't fair on our men and women and we needed to address this. That's what we have done in the last few years and you will see the real difference in the next five when the youngsters who are now growing up start breaking into the national programme. It is a long-term plan and is expected to change the face of Indian hockey in the future.

Boria: When we look at hockey in the state, the other thing that strikes me is how the sport has now become a vehicle of women's empowerment. We see Odisha doing extremely well at all national age group tournaments and there are players from the state in the senior national programme as well. Clearly, the efforts put in have started to show results already.

Dilip: I don't think I will be wrong if I say that in the past few years the girls in Odisha have done better than the boys. In fact, the performances of the girls are a clear index how much they have improved in the last few years. At the junior and sub-junior levels, our girls are in the top bracket nationally and a number of them have made it to the senior Indian national team as well. In Rio, there were more girls than boys in the senior national team. In Tokyo, there were two of our girls from Odisha in the women's team and now we have the extremely talented Anjali in the junior set-up while we have Jyoti and Sunelita in the senior set-up.

I will be candid when I say this to you. I did not expect this level of improvement from our girls. And it is not just a sports story. When you go to the villages and see these girls play hockey, you know that it is far more than a sport that they are playing. Some of these villages have never seen anything beyond farming. The men and women have led lives of struggle. And now thanks to the opportunities provided by the government, young men and women from underprivileged backgrounds have started to dream of a life of comfort because of sport. That's the bigger story of empowerment I am keen on. When sport becomes a means to a better life, that's what you want to see as an administrator. And once it starts, there is no stopping. For years, these women did not have the opportunity. Now they do. They know they have equal opportunity as men and things will only get better. This is one of the best things to happen in Odisha in the last few years.

Vineel: Women's empowerment is one of the fundamental subjects the Honourable Chief Minister has focussed on in the last two decades. We have this project called Mission Shakti under which 70 lakh women are being empowered through Self Help Groups. The sports project is an extension of this overall vision that the state has at the moment. And it is not just restricted to hockey. Rather, it now extends to sports like rugby, gymnastics, athletics and a number of other disciplines. We have documented the story of the rugby girls in this book. When the CM announced 10 lacs as a cash incentive for every athlete participating at the Asian Games for India, it is to encourage many more to play sport. The idea is to make sport a viable career option for our women and that's what we have been able to achieve in the last few years. Playing sport at a professional level is now an opportunity at social mobility and if you do an ethnographic study across disciplines, you will know that women in large numbers have come to sport looking at it as a means to a better life. It is no surprise as Dilip said that our girls are doing as well and if not better than the boys at the moment.

Boria: When you speak of women's empowerment, I also need to ask you about sports opportunities for the disabled. This is one area where we need to do a lot better in India. If you ask someone on the streets today who is Murlikant Petkar you will get a blank stare. You tell the same person do you know Kartik Aryan and he or she will say yes. Then you have to say Kartik Aryan is playing Murlikant Petkar, India's first ever Paralympic Gold medallist back in 1972, in a Kabir Khan film and it will ring a bell. If you travel across India, not even 10 per cent of our sports facilities are disabled-friendly. There are no ramps, no disabled-friendly toilets and the basic facilities are still lacking.

Vineel: I am glad you raised this question for we confront this regularly in all our planning meetings here in Odisha. First, it is a clear mandate from the CM that people with disability or sportsmen and women with disability are to be treated at par with the able-bodied athletes. So in terms of incentives or cash rewards or jobs, which we offer if they win medals, things are all equal for men and women of disability in comparison to the able-bodied athletes. This has now been the case for some years now. We paid six crores to Pramod Bhagat, para badminton gold medallist after the Tokyo Paralympic Games. Coming to facilities for athletes with disability, it was a very conscious decision when building the Birsa Munda Stadium that we will have separate ramps and disable-friendly toilets. This is not just restricted to one stadium. Rather, it is to be done in every facility we build. At the Olympic level, the success of our athletes with disability has made a huge difference to the country. In London 2012, we had won just one medal. In Rio, the number went up to four and in Tokyo it jumped to 19. I am told India is well poised to win close to 35 medals in Paris.

We are conscious that we need to be a part of this growth story and do everything we can to help these athletes. Their struggles and stories offer encouragement to us all. But let me also say, it is not fair to treat them as stories. Rather, they are regular citizens who have equal rights and need facilities similar to what their able-bodied counterparts have. In Odisha at least, this is something we are consciously doing and will continue to do going forward. If you see the number of para sport competitions we have hosted, you will know it is not mere talk. We have supported para athletics, para badminton, para wheelchair fencing and a number of other events in the state.

Dilip: These efforts aren't just restricted to sport. When you treat men and women of disability with respect, it is part of a larger societal change. That's the larger focus for us in Odisha at the moment. We need greater sensitivity in India and that's what we are seeing in Odisha. It is a start for the better.

Boria: One thing is to see elite high-performance sport flourishing. But a completely different thing to see the people of the state get behind the sport to support it. In

Odisha, I see that happening. I see people from diverse backgrounds going to the hockey and enjoy watching the sport. Irrespective of who is playing, there are thousands in the stadium. That's the best advertisement for any sport in any part of the country.

Dilip: I agree with you entirely. Like I said to you at the start of our conversation, people in Odisha love their hockey. They are crazy about hockey in Sundargarh. And you can see that if you go there. Almost every street and by-lane will have kids playing the sport. When we hosted the sub junior competition at the Birsa Munda Stadium there were 7000-8000 people watching. And they were not just watching the Odisha games. Rather they were watching every game and encouraging the players. When I was there, I was hugely impressed to see them applauding every goal irrespective of who was playing. That's when you know the fans love the sport and that's when something major happens.

Take the case of the 2023 World Cup as a case study. Unfortunately for us, India did not make the quarter finals. In any other sport, that would have come as a real blow for the tournament. If the host country loses out, the fans lose interest. It is natural. Sport is about nationalism and this is something that we all know for years. And once the fans lose interest, the broadcaster too finds it difficult to sustain the intensity because they are confronted with empty stands. I was apprehensive it could happen to the World Cup after India lost. But I was wrong and I must say I am very pleased I was! In Rourkela, every single match was sold out. There were 20,000 people in classification matches. In my three decades of being associated with the sport, I have never seen anything like this. When India was playing, there were 23000 people cheering the team without caring for the result. With such a passionate fan base it is no surprise that Odisha is the new home of Indian hockey.

Vineel: What is important to state here is that the fandom is not restricted to the cities. Rather, the idea is to develop sports facilities across the state, which gets more and more people attracted to an active lifestyle. Not everyone will be an elite high-performance sportsperson. It is important that we understand that not everyone needs to be. But what we do need in India is for people to embrace an active lifestyle. Play some form of sport if they can. And it can happen if sport is an integral part of our lives. When you see your heroes playing in front of you, it is automatically something that you want to do or emulate. If the citizens of Rourkela see the Indian hockey stars play in the Birsa Munda Stadium, it is natural that they will want to embrace hockey further. That's how it always is. We have now developed a huge number of grassroot centres across the state so that everyone has access to sports facilities and we can bring about a lifestyle change. You don't have to travel for hours to come to the state capital or a major town to have access. Such things hinder development for only a few can or will ever do so. But if you have an artificial turf in your block, there is a far greater chance of you taking up the sport. With facilities spread far and wide, it is no surprise that we have strong support for hockey in most parts of the state.

What we have also done is build the stadium like a mall. It is to encourage local people in Rourkela to just come and spend a family evening in the facility. That way we will have continuous use of the facility and it won't ever turn into a white elephant in the future.

Boria: I also want to ask you both about the emphasis on fitness. Earlier, it was only about skill development. But now with a very different game, you need highly improved standards of fitness. If I go back to Tokyo, the reason we did well was because Indian teams, both men and women, were perhaps the fittest teams on show. That's something I see here in Odisha. There is a lot of emphasis on fitness and sports science.

Dilip: It was a very conscious move to steer the sport in that direction. Modern hockey is very different to what we were used to seeing in the past. In the fourth quarter, the intensity of the game inevitably picks up. And unless you are fit and focussed you won't be able to keep pace. And here I am not simply referring to physical fitness. Rather, I am referring to physical and mental fitness. Unless you are mentally switched on you will make mistakes in the last minute under pressure. How many times has it happened in the past that Indian teams have conceded a goal in the last two minutes and missed out on major opportunities. We played well throughout the game and then a last-minute mistake cost us the match. It has happened far too many times in the past and we know it. Now things have changed. We don't concede last minute goals. Rather, we score last minute goals. And that's because we are a fitter and more focussed side. It is the result of years of work and Odisha has yet again led the way. You have met and discussed things with David John. His emphasis as HPD has always been on fitness. Unless you are a fit player, you can never succeed in sport at the highest level.

What I am also keen on as president of Hockey India is to improve on our drag-flicking ability. Short corners win you games. You can score goals from short corners and when you concede short corners, you need to save them. And in our team, we have Amit Rohidas from Odisha who is now one of the best first rushers in the world. A large part of what he does can be attributed to his fitness. Defensively he is the best you can have. In Tokyo, Harmanpreet and Rupinder Pal both scored multiple goals for India. I am very keen on organising specialised camps for our players and yet again the facilities that have been made available here in Odisha at the Kalinga Stadium and in Rourkela make it possible for me to do so.

Vineel: I will answer this as a spectator. When we watched the Indian team play say between 2000-2015, we knew that we were never lacking in skill. And yet, we wouldn't win at the international stage. Something clearly was lacking. And the one answer is fitness. We would lose steam towards the end and concede goals in the last few minutes of the game. Each time this would happen, the sport would be pushed back by months and years. You need to do well for your youngsters to feel the encouragement to take up the sport. And it can only happen if your national teams are fit enough to compete with the Europeans and outperform them. That's international sport for you and that's what we have tried to do here in Odisha in all our sub-junior and junior programmes.

Boria: Finally, to you Dilip bhai, we have often seen differences between governments and federations. We have seen egos take over. We have seen fights for control. But here in Odisha, and I am not saying this because the two of you are part of this conversation, I see a kind of seamless synergy. I see positivity and focus. I see red tape not coming in the way of development and that's a fantastic thing. I see people working closely together.

Dilip: We only have words of gratitude for the government. May be because I am a son of the soil, I know what it takes for them to do what they are doing. When the last sponsorship deal for the national teams was coming to an end, Hockey India was struggling to an extent. And then with Covid impacting our lives, things would get really difficult. The Odisha Government coming forward solved everything for us. All of a sudden Hockey India did not have to worry about sponsorship or about raising money and could just focus on improving the sport at all levels. With the government committing to supporting the team for five years, and now it has been extended for a further 10 years, the players have the comfort and the confidence they need to just focus on playing the sport. If they need to worry about money and sponsorship and what will happen to their families, it is never a good feeling. That's where the support from the government has been a huge value add. As

Federation Head I can tell you I don't have to worry day to day because I know I have the support of the Odisha Government. My energies are focussed on making India one of the best in the world and without money and means, it is never possible to do so.

Vineel: Let me add to this. From day one, the Chief Minister, who played hockey as a young man and was a goalkeeper, was clear that we can't equate hockey with any other sport in India. If you go back to the colonial times, hockey was one of the realms where the Indians challenged the British and won against them. It was a symbol of Indian nationalism and was something that allowed colonial India to make its mark at the world stage. Winning multiple gold medals between 1928-1964 is proof how good India was at hockey in colonial and immediate post-colonial India. Thereafter, hockey in India lost some of its sheen and the sport was not in the best health. We did not qualify for the 2008 Beijing Olympics and it was a huge national disappointment. That's why when the last sponsor decided to not continue further, the CM instructed us to go all in. He was clear we had to do everything possible for hockey to regain its lost glory in India. As a result, we decided to sponsor the men's and women's teams and also invested heavily in the junior and sub-junior programmes.

You need to keep something in mind. Unless you

have government support, it is impossible to create world-class infrastructure and host world-class events. Each of these things involve a lot of money and it is not possible for federations or corporates to do these things on their own. We hosted a huge number of hockey events in the last few years because we wanted the sport to get back to its best in India. When you host World Cups and pro league games and other such events, your team gets an opportunity to play in front of home crowds. In front of a 20,000-capacity crowd, they too feel motivated to give it their all. The fact that today India is at number three in the world rankings is also largely because we have helped our team play a number of important games at home. That's how you support the sport and help the federation. Like Dilip said, we need to work in synergy for us to deliver the best results.

Boria: While it is a future driven approach, it is great to see that you haven't forgotten the past. During the World Cup in January 2023, the 1980 Moscow gold medal-winning team was felicitated and the 1975 World Cup-winning side was also here in Bhubaneshwar. The hockey documentary, which was released by the Honourable CM on August 15, 2023 is a celebration of the history of the sport in India. Such things are rarely seen.

Vineel: You can't forget the past and just start to think of the future. Hockey is what it is in India because of the past. That's what the legacy is all about. And we needed to document this story. You want future generations to know who Dilip Tirkey was and what we did for the sport. You need kids to know his story and about Dhyan Chand and Balbir Singh Senior and what they did to get to where they did. None of these things can be seen in isolation. Rather, they are all part of the larger vision that the CM has for sport in the state. Sport for us, as Shri VK Pandian always says, is about values.

Dilip: For a change, let me ask you a question, Boria. You have studied and taught sport across the world. You are a very senior journalist. How do you rate the facilities that you have seen here in Odisha with what you have seen in other parts of the world?

Boria: I am glad you asked me this. I have lived and studied in the UK and Australia and also taught in Canada. And I can tell you with full certainty that I have not seen anything like this Kalinga Stadium precinct in any part of the world. So many different high-performance centres for sport embracing so many diverse disciplines is rare. The sports science facility, which binds them together, is state of the art and there is a kind of thread that stitches all of these little parts together. The planning is fantastic, and this is a one-of-its-kind facility in the world.

Vineel: I will tell you two final things to round off. Sport for us is about values. About a kind of education that students normally don't get in schools. Our hostels are all modelled in a manner that we have sport integrated into the curriculum and vice versa. We have tried to use sport as a means to holistic development for young people in the state. That's what explains our partnership with OVEP. You can teach kids a lot more using sport if you know what I mean. The ethic of fair play, of teamwork, of leadership, can all be taught using sport. And we are not the only state in the country doing this. We continuously send our delegations to other states and try to learn from them. We need to see what they are doing and imbibe the best learnings. We also have multiple delegations from other states visiting us here in Odisha to see what we have done in the last few years and what the Odisha model is all about. Frankly, it is all about partnerships. And if we can replicate the partnerships at a national level, we can all add to the India story. When you watched the world javelin final in Budapest you had three Indians from diverse backgrounds making the final. There was Neeraj Chopra, DP Manu and Kishore Jena. While each is very different, each is also part of the Indian story of sport. Never has it happened that we have seen three Indians in the final of a world athletics event. That's what we want to do here in Odisha. Provide people with opportunities. Help hone their talent in ways that hasn't been done before in the past. That's what the CM wants us to do and that's what each one of us are invested in. Odisha has always been known for its disaster management. We are a bunch of resilient people and are known to never give up. That's what sport is all about. To never give up. We don't want the negative rhetoric surrounding Indian sport to dominate our lives anymore. After every Asian Games or Olympics it is always about the few medals that India has won. We want to change this narrative and that's what we are all trying to do here in Odisha. And in doing so, we also want to create a more healthy and inclusive society, one where sport is all pervasive and seamlessly integrated.

KISHORE JENA, AND AN OLYMPIC DREAM COME TRUE

By the end of the fortnight in Hangzhou, Indian sport had many champions to celebrate. Few, however, have a backstory like Kishore Jena. An unknown when he went to the World Athletics Championships in Budapest in August, he stunned a high-calibre field with a throw of 84.77m that briefly had him in fourth place. He eventually finished fifth behind Neeraj Chopra—India's first athletics world champion—and just 23cm short of the qualifying standard for the Paris Olympics in 2024.

That performance made him a medal contender in Hangzhou, especially once Arshad Nadeem of Pakistan pulled out injured. But few major finals have packed in as much drama and incident as the javelin final at the Asian Games. It is in any case one of the most technical and difficult of events to master, but that night, the athletes' temperament was tested every bit as much as their skill.

It started with Neeraj, Indian athletics' golden boy, throwing close to the Games record, only to rediscover after a delay of more than 15 minutes that he would have to do it all over again. The first fling, for reasons best known to the officials, hadn't been registered. Despite the effect that such a delay would have had on his concentration, Jena threw over 80m to ease into second place. Then, in the second round, his throw was red-flagged, even though the line judge was looking away at some far horizon and not at Jena's feet. It was only after the intervention of Neeraj and others that the white flag was correctly raised.

If the intention was to upset Jena's rhythm or undermine his confidence, it had the opposite effect. In the third round, he stunned those watching with a throw of 86.77m, more than two metres clear of what Neeraj had thrown till then. Not only was his ticket to Paris punched, but a stunning upset and gold medal could be seen on the horizon.

That didn't happen. Neeraj responded with a monster throw of 88.88m, and though Jena went where he had never gone before with a stunning hurl of 87.54 in the same round, the natural order of things had been restored. Neeraj was once more the golden boy, but it was the man who had improved his personal best by close to three metres that was the real story. The next afternoon, we spoke, not long after he had an emotional conversation with his family back home in Odisha.

This is that interview.

Boria: I was in Orissa for two weeks earlier this year, and every day, R. Vineel Krishna and his team would talk to me about one individual—Kishore Jena. He was then training for the World Championships in Budapest, and we saw how he performed there. He couldn't throw the 85m needed for Olympic qualification, but that night in Budapest told us that Puri to Paris could be a reality. And last night in Hangzhou, we saw it happen. Congratulations, you are the athlete of the games. From 78m to over 87.5m. How did it happen?

Kishore Jena: First of all, thank you. I just want to give my 100 per cent in every competition. It happens for you sometimes, it doesn't at other moments. Hopefully, I can post more personal bests and take the country's name even further.

Boria: Tell us a bit more about the support from the Government of Odisha. The Chief Minister has already announced an award of Rupees 1.5 crores for you.

Kishore: Many thanks to the Odisha Government, especially to Chief Minister Naveen Patnaik Sir. See, when someone stands behind you like that, it makes you want to do even more. They're doing an amazing job.

Boria: What was it like to compete with Neeraj Chopra and win medals together? What did you talk about?

Kishore: We were together in Budapest as well, and his experience came in very useful. In Budapest, we were three [DP Manu as well]. Here, we were two [in the final]. And Neeraj Bhai was telling me I was throwing well. And in between, we kept encouraging each other to do better. And Neeraj Bhai had told me even before that I would return with a medal. When throwing, you don't focus so much on the other person. But it was fun out there with him.

Boria: After the event, you got Indian flags from Anju Bobby George, draped them around you and then went to celebrate together and take photographs. Tell us about that feeling.

Kishore: At that time, it felt like there was nothing left to do but have fun and enjoy it. It's hard to describe.

Boria: And when the flag was going up [during the medal ceremony] and the national anthem was being played, tell us about that feeling?

Kishore: I can't even tell you how that felt, standing on the podium. That feeling is indescribable.

Boria: Kishore, Puri to Paris. Even in 2021-2022, you were throwing 77-78m. From there, to improve 10m… take me backstage. What kind of training has gone into it? Tell me about the motivation and the effort that has gone into it. Because it's a story of what's possible. You have shown that.

Kishore: While training, I paid a lot of attention to technique. In javelin, the focus has to be on that. It's a light object and throwing it long distances is difficult. It's about angles and speeds, that's what we focus on. Initially, at national level, I'd be afraid. But with experience, that has gone. At the international level, I've just started out. The more I compete, the more experienced I'll get, and you'll be able to see even better things in Paris.

Boria: My team and I will be in Paris to support you on August 7 and 8 [2024]. Tell me a bit about the Olympics.

Kishore: I don't have a target in mind, but I will give my best. I know if I throw my personal best, I could win a medal.

Boria: Right now, your personal best is close to 88m. If you throw that, you should get a medal. Fingers crossed.

Kishore: Certainly. My full effort will be directed at that.

Boria: When Neeraj's first throw was cancelled, at that time…how difficult is it for an athlete?

Kishore: It was a great throw, about 88 to 89m. I had gone and asked him what was happening. Our Chief Coach was also there. We were all trying to figure out what had happened. I think there was some problem with the measurement. They told him they hadn't been able to measure it and he would get another chance. Such things do disturb an athlete. Otherwise, maybe the Asian Games record would have gone.

Boria: You told the media that you had a lot of debts that you wanted to clear first with the money you're earning. Tell us a bit about that. People like you shouldn't struggle. You're the nation's pride, the one-per centers. I'm pleased that the support has come from the Government of Odisha, as well as the Government of India and SAI (Sports Authority of India).

Kishore: For even those from the middle class, it's difficult to move forward once you reach a certain stage. But the Odisha Government stood by me, and emboldened me to do even better. So, I want to thank them for the reward, and I'll do even better in Paris.

Boria: And celebrations? Paris is still some way off. There must have been some celebrations with Neeraj?

Kishore: We got back quite late, around 1am. We sat with three or four friends for a while and then went to sleep.

Boria: And when you got home? Did you talk to your family?

Kishore: I spoke to them after many days. We have a small phone at home. You can't do video calls on that, just normal calls. But today, my father's elder brother's son made a video call. So, I was able to talk to them this morning.

Boria: And tell us about that? What happened?

Kishore: What can I say about that? They were just crying at home. I haven't been home for a while. Hopefully, I'll get the chance to go and see them now.

A STORY OF HOPE AND OPTIMISM

R. Vineel Krishna

The one fundamental question I have asked of myself since starting my career as a civil servant is what difference am I able to make to the people and will I leave my state in a better place after I move on from my position?

When you are a government servant, it is never about you as an individual. We work as a collective and it is always about us as 'government'. This is an everyday reality for us in Odisha. Whatever we have been able to achieve in the last six years is because we worked as a team. Even when the chips were down because of Covid, we did not give up. We did feel the stress during the organisation of the 2023 Hockey World Cup. With supply chain disruptions around the world delaying work, it was hugely difficult for everyone involved. But that's when the spirit came to the fore. No one blamed the other. Rather, each one of us stood up for our colleagues and played on as a team. That's what explains the successful organisation of the event and that's what has set us apart.

Inspired by the vision and guidance of our Chief Minister, Shri Naveen Patnaik, we are all invested in using sport to showcase Odisha in front of the world. We seek satisfaction in creating infrastructure of the very highest global standard, which has subsequently helped and continue to help our athletes in trying to be the best they can and prepare the best for global competitions.

The CM, a sports lover and one who played hockey while growing up, believes that sport has the power to unite and help bring about positive change. He is committed to reviving the glory days of hockey and make India a world champion in hockey again. He wants to see our men and women, boys and girls on the podium and that's what he has repeatedly harped on in every conversation with us. In colonial India, it was hockey, which had given us a voice. It was an arena where India played and beat the British and made a statement to the world. Beating Germany in front of Adolf Hitler in Berlin in 1936 or beating Great Britain in London in 1948 are huge nationalist moments in our history. These wins tell a story of what India was capable of. In fact, the multiple

Olympic gold medals won between 1928-1964 are proof of Indian dominance and yet between 1984 and 2021 India did not win a single Olympic medal in the sport. That's what we wanted to change. And it happened in Tokyo for the men after 41 years. The women too were close having stunned world champions Australia in the quarter final and were unlucky in the end.

As the CM says, such change can only come about if we back our teams with infrastructure, coaching and monetary support. Guided by this belief, we decided to sponsor the teams, both men and women, first for five years and have now renewed it for a further 10 till 2033. We have also created the best infrastructure through our high performance and grassroot centres, which are all focussed on fitness and skill development and offer the best coaching in partnership with the corporates who have experience in the domain.

As I write, the Indian men's team is ranked No. 3 in the world and is capable of taking on and beating any European side. We have won the Asian Champions Trophy, Hangzhou Asian Games Gold Medal and are poised to do well in the Paris 2024 Olympics. That's where we seek vindication. While we won't go out there and play, what we will do is empower. Ensure that our teams are the fittest and prepare the best and are also the best equipped to face the challenges head on. By creating the Birsa Munda Stadium, the world's best hockey stadium with a capacity of 23,000, we have made a statement. Odisha is the home of world and Indian hockey, and it houses the best facilities for the sport. When our teams train in Rourkela or Kalinga, they have access to the best templates that sports science can offer and we can see the impact in the improved fitness of both our men's and women's teams.

Also, none of our facilities are restricted to the senior programmes. Rather, the emphasis is on the sub-juniors and juniors for they are the ones who will graduate into the senior programme in the next five years. In 2022-2023 Odisha has produced its best ever performance in the nationals for sub-juniors and juniors and each of our junior teams have access to modern technology for fitness and skill development.

The Chief Minister was clear in his mandate—we have to do everything possible to help the sport. And that's what we have done. We have created the Birsa Munda Stadium and the adjoining World Cup village with quality residential facilities, we have upgraded the Kalinga Stadium and made it one of the best in the world, set up the HPC with the Tatas and recruited David John, one of the best HPD's in the world, as the man in charge. And the changes are already noticeable. Players from Odisha are breaking into the national programmes, both junior and senior, and some like Sunelita Toppo is already being hailed as the next major Indian hockey star.

While the world knows us now for our hockey, it is no longer restricted to just one sport. The state has made giant strides in athletics, weightlifting, sports science, shooting, swimming and rugby. We have also built a state of the art aquatics centre and India's first indoor athletics stadium.

In Odisha, it is not just talk. The CM has often asked what's the best way to showcase our commitment to sport? How is it that the country will recognise we are serious with what we are trying to do? And the best way to do so is by allocating funds for sport in the state budget. Today the amount of money earmarked is touching 1300 crores. That's a 30-fold jump compared to where we were a decade and a half earlier. With the state taking the lead, it is natural that our corporate partners look at us as sincere and committed and have all stepped forward in working together for the cause of Indian sport. The public-private partnership, which is at the core of the Odisha model, has now evolved into a successful template, which is being replicated in other parts of the country. We as government provide the infrastructure and funds to build the facilities while the corporate partners bring in the coaching and high-quality technical expertise. With a vision that has the athlete at its core, results have started to show. The rise of Kishore Jena in men's javelin, the presence of multiple players from Odisha in the Indian women's rugby team, growing representation in the men's and women's national programmes for hockey, consistent improvement in weightlifting and athletics are all indicative of progress in the right direction.

However, it is not just about elite sport. Can never be. Not more than one per cent of our people will make it to the national teams. Rather, the vision is always guided by the principle of sport for all and sport for development. You don't need to be a national level athlete to access the facilities. Such a policy ends up being restrictive and is an obstacle for all round development. Guided by the principle of sports for all, we have made the Birsa Munda Stadium accessible for the local people for a large part of the year. We have opened hundreds of grassroot centres in every part of the state with state-of-the-art indoor stadiums so that people never feel stifled by the lack of opportunity. Playing sport is a kind of lifestyle change that we have tried to bring about in the state. A fitter India will always be a better India and that's what we have tried to achieve in Odisha.

There have been many challenges on the way. And there will be many more in the future. Odisha for the longest time was not the favoured destination for the best professionals to come and work in. They would prefer cities like Delhi, Mumbai or Bengaluru instead. Now things are changing. From young management students to already established professionals, all realise that Odisha is a hotbed of opportunity. That we take our sport seriously and will continue to do important work in the realm. According to a recent report published by the RBI, Odisha is now a favoured investment destination and the way the state has been looked upon in the past is changing at breakneck speed.

Last words

Indian sport is on the cusp. If recent trends are anything to go by Indian stars are now winning medals in almost every international competition across sports or at least coming close. And this includes both able-bodied and para sports.

In hockey, we are now in the world's top 3 teams. Badminton has seen a sea change in the last decade. The TT effort isn't bad either. Boxing, both men and women, have started to look up and shooting too is on an upswing. Athletics has been the shining light with many national records rewritten in the last few months, not to mention Neeraj Chopra making it to the very top in world javelin. Football is seeing a wave of support come its way and in chess, India has turned a new leaf with the golden generation. The fundamental reason why this is now a reality is because there is a lot more money in sport. In Odisha, for example, with direct intervention from the CM, sport is now a priority for the government and the results have started to show.

On the positive side of the ledger, the funding for sports, nationally as well, has increased. In early 2016, India was spending about Rs 11.5 per Indian on sports (with about Rs 1,541 crore in the union sports budget). By 2019, this spending had increased to Rs 16.5 per Indian (with an overall sports budget of Rs 2,216.92 crore). And the last union budget further added to the quota allocated for sport by a few hundred crores.

In Odisha, we started with a meagre 50-crore budget at the turn of the millennium. Now our sports budget is a staggering 1300 crores.

Second, there is a lesson to draw from cricket, which grew as a business because of the money that television brought into the game. Cricket reigns supreme in India, but in the last few years, the country's market size for Olympic sports has also grown significantly. The industry's size expanded from $1.7 billion in 2013 to about $2.7 billion in 2018 and is now approximately 6-7 billion in 2023. This is important because sporting infrastructure requires money. In 2018, the Managing Director of Star

India at the time, Sanjay Gupta, told the Confederation of Indian Industry's (CII) Scorecard forum that the sports industry's size can expand to about $10 billion by 2024. 'Over the last few years, the kind of activity around the business of sports has been tremendous,' he pointed out. 'There are now over 15 domestic leagues in the country—across kabaddi, football, kho kho, badminton—from just two, five years back.' When television starts focusing on sports and creating stars, it has a knock-on effect in terms of aspiration. In the case of badminton, as Gopichand points out, the catchment area has increased. 'I think what used to be about 30 or 40 players in numbers has actually gone up to around 2,000-2,500,' he says. 'So, the number of people playing the game seriously has increased by maybe 100-200 per cent every year in the last few years, especially in the 13-to-15-year sub-junior categories. These are amazing numbers and the quality of players who are playing at a certain level has gone up as well. Earlier, there were maybe ten kids who could actually play a serious rally. That number has gone to many thousands now. So, I think, the overall standard of grassroots-level badminton has grown drastically.'

And all this has been possible because of the money that has come into sport. Rewards have grown exponentially for medal winners and sports stars now earn considerable wealth in the course of a successful career. Take the case of Neeraj Chopra. He is now one of India's highest-paid stars who charges just second to Virat Kohli for endorsement fees. Chopra received nearly 25 crores in the form of rewards after winning a gold medal in Tokyo and is now one of India's most sought after celebrities. The same applies to PV Sindhu. Her two Olympic medals have made her one of India's best-known global stars and these athletes now come close to film personalities in terms of earnings.

What is also a welcome sign is how some states like ours have appropriated sports and are now investing considerable wealth in creating world class infrastructure. By doing so, we have been able to tap into the latent talent pool in India, which has always lost out in the absence of adequate opportunities. In rural or tribal belts for example, it is always about the basics of food and shelter. If sport can help these men and women improve their lives, there is little doubt, they'd encourage the children to pursue sport. And with the athleticism and talent, which some of these kids are born with, they can surely be the success stories of the future.

To close with a story that is very close to my heart. Just 36 hours before the start of the Asian Athletics Championship in July 2017, which marked the start of our sports journey in Odisha, it started to rain incessantly in Bhubaneshwar. The last-minute preparations were badly impacted and we had to cancel the dress rehearsals for the opening ceremony. Each one of us was nervous. We were all praying for the rains to relent so that we could get on with the show. With enormous work already done, we needed this to happen. And it did. Miraculously, the rain stopped and it all went ahead smoothly. So much so the competition was hailed as the best ever with India topping the medals tally. The Doha organisers, who were to host the next edition of the competition, were in awe and it felt like the ultimate vindication of sorts. Little did we know that it was just the start. Today when we write this book, it seems a journey worth the effort. But then, this book is also a reminder. It tells us what we can do as a collective, and how it can help India make a mark in the global sporting amphitheatre. A dream that started when Shri VK Pandian had first mentioned the idea to the Hon CM in 2017 is now a full grown reality. Odisha is now recognised as one of the key states in the Indian sports story. 'We have been through difficult times. We have dealt with Covid. But at no point did we lose hope and never did we give up on our commitment to promote and develop Indian sport', said Shri Pandian.

As I conclude this chapter, I have the pleasure in saying that we have just hosted the legendary, Arsene Wenger, FIFA's global chief of football development, to start off a dedicated a premier talent harnessing academy that will be managed by the world governing body of the sport—FIFA—in collaboration with AIFF and the Government of Odisha.

Arsene Wenger has suggested that the academy, which will be called AIFF-FIFA Talent Academy, should focus on scouting talents at the right age and prepare players for future Indian teams. We have now formalised it with the signing of a Memorandum of Understanding with the AIFF President Kalyan Chaubey and Arsene Wenger on behalf of FIFA.

To go back to the words of the Honourable Chief Minister one final time: 'Sport for youth and youth for future'. That's the Odisha sports story—one of optimism, aspiration and hope. Most importantly, an attempt to make a difference.

Acknowledgements

We would like to thank the Hon Chief Minister Shri Naveen Patnaik, Shri VK Pandian, Sports Minister Shri Tushar Kanti Behera, members of the Sports Department of the Government of Odisha and Dipta Mishra, Hockey India, President Dilip Tirkey and every player, men and women, who we had the pleasure of speaking to, members of the Abhinav Bindra Foundation, Abhinav Bindra, Rahul Bose and Rugby India, Kishore Jena, Adille Sumariwla and the Athletics Federation of India, Reliance Foundation and James Hillier, David John, Rajiv Seth and every stakeholder who helped us in piecing together this story.

Our thanks to our publishers, Simon and Schuster India, Rahul Srivastava, Sayantan Ghosh, and our designer Rajinder Ganju.

This book is for every Indian fan who believe in the power of sport and every citizen of Odisha who are stakeholders in this narrative of transformation.